PRAISE FOR
RESPONSIVE FUNDRAISING

"In *Responsive Fundraising*, Gabe names the challenging and uncomfortable realities facing nonprofit organizations and their fundraising efforts. And, he offers the philosophical and tactical changes nonprofits will need to make to thrive in this rapidly changing environment."

CHRIS HORST
Chief Advancement Officer at
HOPE International and Author

"*Responsive Fundraising* is a must-have for nonprofits seeking to build authentic relationships with donors. Gabe and team provide practical, technology-forward tactics for listening to your donors and then building personal connections at scale."

NICOLE JOHANSSON
VP Advancement, OneHope, Inc.

"Part manifesto, part guidebook and full of stories that highlight the possibilities that being responsive in our fundraising can bring. This book should be on every fundraiser's shelf, dog-eared, highlighted, underlined and referenced frequently as a guide for a truly comprehensive, donor-centered approach."

T. CLAY BUCK
CFRE

"*Responsive Fundraising* is an essential handbook for modern nonprofits. It provides practical help for growing generosity by focusing on the needs of individual donors."

JOHN RUHLIN
Author of Giftology

"*Responsive Fundraising* represents a sea-change for how most nonprofits think about fundraising. The simple 3-step methodology lays out a roadmap for combining technology, data-intelligence and marketing strategy to accelerate generosity. A must-read for any nonprofit that seeks to engage the modern donor."

TIM KARCHURIAK
Chief Innovation and Optimization Officer, NextAfter

"*Responsive Fundraising* is essential reading for any fundraiser hoping to turn hard-earned attention into action in our hyper-connected world."

CURT STEINHORST
Bestselling author of *Can I Have Your Attention?*

RESPONSIVE
FUNDRAISING

THE DONOR-CENTRIC FRAMEWORK HELPING
TODAY'S LEADING NONPROFITS
GROW GIVING

RESPONSIVE FUNDRAISING

THE DONOR-CENTRIC FRAMEWORK HELPING TODAY'S LEADING NONPROFITS GROW GIVING

GABE COOPER
and
MCKENNA BAILEY

liberalis

ACKNOWLEDGEMENTS

First, I'd like to thank the team at Virtuous for helping make *Responsive Fundraising* a reality. Specific thanks to Noah Barnett, Ben Snedeker, David Cady, Gregg Scoresby, Troy Henikoff, and Mckenna Bailey, who've helped support Virtuous and bring the concept of *Responsive Fundraising* to life.

A big thanks to all the amazing fundraisers, technologists and nonprofit marketers that I've worked with for the last 15 years. You've helped mold, refine and prove these ideas. I'm simply standing on the shoulders of giants. I'd especially like to thank Brad Davies, Stephen Boudreau, Chris Meschner, Tim Kachuriak and NextAfter, Dave Raley and team Dunham for your amazing wisdom and friendship through the years.

A special thanks to our early customers at Virtuous including OneHope, Equitas, and St Joseph the Worker, who were willing to take a risk, believe in our approach, and support us along the way.

Finally, thank you to my amazing family and friends who've supported me endlessly, including Brian MacKay, Brad Routh, Sam Hoefer, Wade, Corey, and the M1 community. Also, to my parents, my amazing wife, Farrah, and my kids who model truly selfish.

TABLE OF CONTENTS

WHY I WROTE THIS BOOK

"We make a living by what we get, but we make a life by what we give."
— *Winston Churchill*

As humans, we are wired to serve and love each other. In fact, I believe generosity is one of the greatest forces in our culture. When someone chooses to give their time, talent or money, they make a decision to set aside their own interests and prioritize the needs of their neighbor. And there is no greater example of that than the act of selfless generosity. Those who receive the gift are changed, but the giver also feels an internal shift.

I have five kids, from seventeen down to five years old. One of the first things I learned as a parent was how truly selfish I was. It took about six months as a new dad for me to realize my children would not care how much sleep I got, or if I was caught up on my favorite TV series. They required my undivided love and attention. And, because I love them, I was generous with both.

Don't get me wrong. I certainly haven't been a perfect dad. But over time I have learned to set aside my own interests for the interests of my kids and I have seen myself change in tremendous ways because of these daily sacrifices.

This is where generosity starts for many of us — in the seemingly automatic act of giving to those in our daily life. We were given an unearned gift by a parent, or a friend, or a coach, or a teacher. We experienced the power of generosity and then we reciprocated that generosity with those closest to us. Generosity begets generosity.

As we grow, we can't help but notice the needs of those outside of our immediate circle and our generosity spreads to our local community and then to our global network. We are drawn to opportunities to give back; to be part of something bigger than ourselves.

When I decided to start my company, Virtuous, my driving motivation was to help increase generosity worldwide. After fifteen years working for and with nonprofits, I understood that generosity had the power to create amazing good in the world while re-shaping the heart of the giver, compounding what's possible in philanthropy. When generosity grows, we are all elevated. I recognized the transformative power of giving and I wanted to find a way to give back to those organizations that had given so much to me.

Nonprofits serve a critical role in society. They provide givers with opportunities to do good at a scale that would be impossible on their own. My experience of working in the trenches with nonprofits was rewarding and fulfilling. But, nonprofit work can also be incredibly challenging. No matter what nonprofit

I worked with, the same obstacles kept blocking our progress. At the heart of the problem are two pervasive beliefs among nonprofits. First, nonprofits tend to be risk-averse. That is, they believe that the safe choice is always better than a bold, strategic change. And the second belief was that fundraising is a necessary evil in the nonprofit world. Donors are nothing but a means to an end. While our for-profit counterparts evolved under market pressures and desperately worked to serve their customers, most nonprofits were trapped by an institutional inertia that pushed back on innovation and diminished the value of the donors they worked so hard to find.

I watched as fundraisers sent thousands of traditional direct mail pieces that resulted in dropping response rates, which fell faster every year. Month after month, despite every indication that they should be doing things differently, they still chose to use the same tactics with the same donors. It worked in the past, why wouldn't it work now? These were smart people who were committed to doing incredible work, but when it came to fundraising, they were trapped by a legacy model that inhibited their ability to do more good in the world.

What's worse, this traditional model prevented nonprofits from serving the donors whose lives and passions were deeply connected to the cause. Most donors loved our work, but felt alienated by the impersonal — and often desperate — communication they received from our nonprofit.

At Virtuous, we help reimagine fundraising for nonprofits. We believe that many of the traditional approaches to fundraising were designed for a world that no longer exists. Today's donors expect (and deserve) an authentic connection to the cause. But many nonprofits are failing to deliver.

We've seen nonprofits who are thoughtful and generous with their donors inspire a lifetime of sacrificial generosity. They embody the principles of what we call, responsive fundraising. In The Responsive Framework, nonprofits aren't focused solely on their cause; they are also focused on forming the heart of their donors. When done well, responsive fundraising can multiply a nonprofit's impact. Donors become loyal megaphones for the cause, and nonprofits create a true movement that is able to do far more good.

I know that we'll never be able serve every nonprofit through Virtuous. But the principles that we encourage and the strategies we facilitate have the ability to transform fundraising at any organization. That's where the idea for this book was born.

This book aims to define responsive fundraising and establish a framework to help nonprofits inspire meaningful donor relationships and increased generosity. No matter what tools you use or insights you uncover about your donors, The Responsive Framework gives you the foundation you need to connect with today's donor and prime you to adapt to the needs of donors in the future.

The Responsive Framework we have created is simple enough that any organization can easily implement it, yet has tremendous implications for how nonprofits can maximize their impact.

The Responsive Framework can help free your nonprofit from the confines of legacy fundraising tactics and push you towards agile, adaptive strategies that are required for connecting with the modern donor.

The responsive approach to fundraising provides the personal connection and impactful relationships donors desire. The result is predictable, sustainable generosity at a reduced cost to the nonprofit.

Use this book to understand the philosophies behind the responsive fundraising, to see examples of how it is happening in the industry and to carve a path for doing the same in your own organization.

The first section of the book lays out the generosity crisis facing today's nonprofits and the changing expectations of today's donors. The next section walks you through The Responsive Framework and provides practical help for treating all of your donors like major donors. Finally, we'll finish with some practical case studies and tactics to help you imagine how responsive might apply at your organization.

Throughout the book, you'll notice boxes we've titled Responsive Plays. These are the practical ways your nonprofit can start integrating responsive fundraising strategies right now. Many of the Plays require technology and practices that might be new to your organization. I've attempted to explain these new practices as thoroughly as possible, but fully embracing these tactics will require hard work and research. Trust me, the hard work will be worth it. The Responsive Plays and practices shared in this book can be used as a foundation transforming your nonprofit into a responsive organization. But to ensure they resonate with your specific donors, use your creativity to optimize or adapt them in a way your donors will love.

My hope is that in these pages you'll find the information you need to do the work you're meant to do. Your donors deserve it. Your beneficiaries need it. Here's to your success.

GABE COOPER, 2020

CHAPTER 1:

THE GENEROSITY CRISIS

"No one can see a bubble That's what makes it a bubble."

— *The Big Short*

You may not know John Antioco by name, but there's a good chance you're familiar with his biggest mistake. In early 2000, Antioco took a meeting with a couple of business owners named Reed Hastings and Marc Randolph. The pair were unknowns at the time, but they were hoping to convince Antioco to buy their business for $50 million. Some familiar with the meeting, and the proposal, remember Antioco practically laughing Hasting and Randolph out of the room.[1]

At the time, Antioco couldn't see any upside to buying the struggling start-up. He was in charge of a huge corporation that was a staple of American culture. Hastings and Randolph's small business, on the other hand, was far from financially successful. Without any

---

1   https://variety.com/2013/biz/news/epic-fail-how-blockbuster-could-have-owned-netflix-1200823443/

real incentive, Antioco passed. Unfortunately, by 2010, Antioco's company had declared bankruptcy and Hastings and Randolph found themselves running a multi-billion dollar company.

For those who haven't Googled it yet, Antioco is the former CEO of Blockbuster, and Hastings and Randolph are the co-founders of Netflix.

Media companies love this story, especially in the tech space. It solidifies the lore of visionaries and encourages people to keep pushing, even if no one else appreciates their ideas. For me, the more important lesson in this story is about Antioco. At the time, his decision to pass on Netflix wasn't negligent. Netflix only offered a mail-order DVD service — and more importantly, they were losing money. Antioco already had a partnership lined up with DirecTV that was projected to be an early version of on-demand movie streaming. On paper, his decision looks relatively sound.

But, of course, business decisions involve more than simply what's on paper. In hindsight, we all know that Antioco made a mistake. But his mistake wasn't turning down the early version of Netflix. His biggest mistake had nothing to do with Netflix. Antioco failed Blockbuster when he missed the changes in customer behaviors. The moment he ignored signs that the future would be different than the past, he created a problem that his company would never recover from.

Today, anyone can see that paying $50 million for Netflix was a steal. The new normal of a personalized, on-demand movie selection viewable from any device makes Blockbuster's brick and mortar model of video rental seem ludacris. But noticing the bubble after it bursts isn't helpful. To succeed in an ever-changing culture of technology and human behavior, you've got to be able to see the bubble while it's forming.

THE UNSEEN NONPROFIT BUBBLE

John Antioco's story isn't simply a humorous example of one man turning down a billion-dollar idea. Rather, it serves as a cautionary tale for other industries facing innovation. I lead with his mistake because I don't want to stand by and watch the same thing happen to nonprofits.

Right now, nonprofits are living in a bubble that's primed to pop, and only a few people seem to be paying attention.

On the outside, giving in the United States looks healthier than ever before. From 2006 to 2015, donations in the United States increased from $281 billion to $373 billion.[2] That's almost $10 billion in new generosity added every year. But, if you look a little closer at the numbers, you'll see they tell a different story — one that puts a lot of nonprofits at risk. Over the same period, the number of individual donors dropped by 18 percent. Just under one-fifth of individual donors disappeared. And a deeper dive into the data shows that nonprofits have lost a full 25 percent of their mid- and low-tier donors over the past decade.

We also know that from 2003 to 2013, itemized charitable deductions decreased by 34 percent among those making less than $100,000. This trend continues. In 2018, overall giving increased by 1.5 percent, but donor retention, new donor numbers, repeat

---

2   Generosity For Life. Indiana University: Lilly Family School of Philanthropy. http://generosityforlife.org/generosity-data/fact-sheets/.

donor retention, reactivation rates, and gifts under $1,000? All down.[3]

Nicholas Ellinger perfectly summarizes the issue in his book, *The New Nonprofit,* saying, "If our new donor numbers are down, our overall retention is down, our retention of new donors, specifically, is down, and our recapture rates are down, where are the major donors of the future going to come from?"

It's hard to overstate the implications of that kind of loss. In the last decade, the bottom has dropped out of American generosity, but no one is talking about it. One reason for the silence is the fact that many nonprofits haven't yet felt the pain. Giving from major donors has covered the deficit. Large gifts account for most of the overall revenue growth over the last ten years. This trend is typical in seasons of economic security. Nonprofits can survive on what they receive from major donors. But what happens when major donors can no longer cover the gap?

Even worse: if nonprofits do recognize the bursting bubble, most don't know how to respond. Nonprofit professionals feel the stress of losing individual donors, but they haven't identified *why* donors are leaving in droves every year — or *how* to stop the bleeding. Some nonprofit leaders will argue that people are becoming less generous, but the problem is not a decline in generosity.

---

3 "Fundraising Effectiveness Project Quarterly Fundraising Report™." Association of Fundraising Professionals. https://afpglobal.org/sites/default/files/attachments/2019-02/FEP2018Q4Report.pdf.

In fact, Millennials are more generous than previous generations and, on aggregate, Americans have more to give than ever before.[4]

The fundamental problem is that the fundraising strategies used by most nonprofits were designed for a world that no longer exists. Nonprofits are trying to fit outdated models into a world that has radically changed. And like Antioco, nonprofits are ignoring this shift at the precise moment they should be evolving with it.

Change is constant. Trends, styles, technology, and cultural norms shift every day. Sometimes it happens suddenly, like the first time you were able to FaceTime your friend across the globe or the first time you streamed you favorite pop song on demand.

More often, though, change happens slowly — in ways that are much harder to notice. One night you update your phone's operating system, and everything seems to be the same. Maybe you notice a new feature or two, but, generally speaking, the update seems unnecessary. However, after five or six of these updates, you realize that your phone now tracks your screen time, knows your habits, monitors your health, and even suggests that you put it down for the day when you've scrolled for too long. And, slowly, these seemingly inconsequential changes add up to life-changing shifts. Despite the elongated timeline, the implications are just as significant.

That's how the disconnect between nonprofits and their individual donors has grown in the last ten years. Slowly, but dramatically. And we can't keep ignoring it.

---

4   Brigid Schulte. "Millennials are actually more generous than anybody realizes," The Washington Post, June 24, 2015, https://www.washingtonpost.com/news/wonk/wp/2015/06/24/millennials-are-actually-more-generous-than-anybody-realizes/?noredirect=on

THE DOWNSIDE OF A SOCIAL WORLD

It was no coincidence that the decline in donors began in 2006. In the mid-2000s, platforms like Facebook, Twitter, and even Yelp brought people together around shared experiences. And in 2008, the iPhone made those personalized experiences available anytime, anywhere. Instead of relying on polished commercials and advertisements, people could now learn about any brand or social cause from a diverse set of people and data sources around the world. And this grassroots, community-driven reality spread like wildfire.

Suddenly, generous, thoughtful companies were advocated for in a completely new way. Smaller companies with a focus on transparency and customer service could find new customers simply through reviews, social posts, and offline conversations. At the same time, established companies like Enron, Comcast, Volkswagen, and Citibank saw how a hyper-connected world of customers who felt mistreated, taken advantage of, or even harmed, could hold them accountable in ways they hadn't seen in the past.

Nonprofits were just as vulnerable. The Red Cross, one of the most well-established and well-known organizations in the country, was forced to regain trust with donors because of their "chaotic and inequitable"[5] response to Hurricane Katrina relief. No matter what the industry, it's obvious that more and more individuals are losing trust in established institutions, even ones with altruistic purposes.

---

5   Associated Press. "Despite huge Katrina relief, Red Cross criticized," NBCNEWS.com, September 28,2005. http://www.nbcnews.com/id/9518677/ns/us_news-katrina_the_long_road_back/t/despite-huge-katrina-relief-red-cross-criticized/#.XYzSPpNKhTY.

In previous decades, organizations might have offered occasional public statements, downplaying the gross neglect of trust in an effort to promote "transparency". But in the era of digital media, social sharing, and constant connectivity, there is nowhere to hide. Businesses and nonprofits must maintain a higher level of transparency, cultivate a deeper trust, and reach out to each customer in an authentic, personalized way, if they want to keep them.

OUR NEW REALITY

Mckenna is a member of the Virtuous team and a self-described "quintessential Millennial." She spends a lot of time thinking and writing about technology and culture. I asked her to describe the world of donors in their twenties to mid-thirties. Here's what she had to say:

> *The first thing our generation learned was this world wasn't made for us. We were pre-teens when teachers rolled TVs into our classrooms to show us what terrorism looked like in real-time. As years passed, we watched again and again as grown-ups failed to protect us in schools or elsewhere. Adults told us our career success hinged on attending the right college, but we wouldn't be able to graduate unless we assumed tens of thousands of dollars in debt at 18 years old. If we managed to graduate, the financial crisis made it impossible to get hired or paid a living wage. In short, we couldn't trust much of what was established by the previous generation.*
>
> *At the same time, we learned that there was an online world bending over backwards for our convenience.*

We used the internet to share music with strangers, effectively dismantling the entire music industry. We changed modern celebrities from untouchable, unrelatable mega-stars to niche influencers who looked like us, liked what we liked and we couldn't wait to talk to our friends about it. Essentially, we figured out how to curate a hyper-personalized online life that highlighted everything we loved and ignored the rest.

The shift that Mckenna touched on didn't just happen for Millennials. They might have been the first to adopt new innovations, but the changes have infiltrated everyone's daily lives. In fact, as I sit on my couch typing this, my TV suggests a new show to binge, my Chrome browser uses my streaming behavior to send me a notification for a concert in Phoenix it knows I'll like, and my Ring doorbell app just alerted me of a suspicious car in my neighborhood. The constant connected, hyper-personalized communication is inescapable.

This level of personalization is possible thanks to the huge sets of data collected from our behavior every day. Terabytes of information are gathered from individuals based on where we click online, what we open, what we engage with, and who our friends are. The data is combined with in-store buying habits, location, demographic, and marketing data to compile a robust picture of each of us. And it happens instantaneously.

The result is that my refrigerator knows when I need milk, my pizza place remembers I like black olives, and the Wells Fargo ATM I visit weekly knows the withdrawal I am most likely to make as soon as I insert my debit card.

As each new hyper-personalized experience enters our lives, we feel a little shocked by what is possible. But, after the initial shock wears off, we love the convenience of feeling like all our favorite organizations are working overtime to cater to our needs. We get frustrated when companies or nonprofits don't seem to know what we want. Worse, we abandon them for a more intentional company.

What for-profit companies have figured out is that our connected world has given individuals unprecedented power over their buying (and giving) decisions. Organizations must work incredibly hard to create a unique experience for people if they want to earn attention or recruit supporters. *Harvard Business Review* writers Nicolaj Siggelkow and Christian Terwiesch put it this way:

> *Thanks to new technologies that enable frequent, low-friction, customized digital interactions, companies today are building much deeper ties with customers than ever before. Instead of waiting for customers to come to them, firms are addressing customers' needs the moment they arise — and sometimes even earlier. It's a win-win: Through what we call connected strategies, customers get a dramatically improved experience, and companies boost operational efficiencies at lower costs.* [6]

These connected strategies also help to improve trust between individuals and the organizations that compete for their attention.

---

6   Nicolaj Siggelkow and Christian Terwiesch, "The Age of Continuous Connection," May-June 2009. https://hbr.org/2019/05/the-age-of-continuous-connection.

Eroded institutional trust is one of the hallmarks of the Millennial experience. And just as curated, personalized experiences spread to other generations, so too did the need for organizations to earn trust with all of their constituents.

And this couldn't be more true for nonprofits.

FUNDRAISING NEEDS TO CHANGE

When Travis Kalanick founded Uber, he envisioned an elite black car service that he could rely on. As a busy tech professional in San Francisco, he grew tired of waiting for taxis that were as unreliable as they were run-down. He combined the technology of GPS and the luxury of personal drivers to create an unmatched experience for his customers. With the Uber app, users always knew where the car was, who was driving, and how long before they arrived at their destination.

Uber quickly found success as the most reliable (and democratized) black car service. The company spread across the world, fundamentally changing the way people move. Kalanick had found his blue ocean. Then Lyft arrived, answering the demands of people who wanted the reliability, safety, and visibility of Uber, but didn't need the exclusivity of a black car.

Suddenly, Kalanick had a choice to make. He could focus on a select group of people who preferred extravagant transportation or he could grow his company exponentially by serving a wider customer base. Kalanick, perennially focused on growth, chose the latter. He opened the exclusive experience of his app to everyone. Now, users everywhere can choose the experience they want. Whether they want to carpool with others or order an exclusive black car, everyone can experience an easy, dependable, safe ride. And Kalanick is a billionaire today for that decision.

Why do I bring up Kalanick? Because he did exactly what donors are asking of you and your nonprofit right now. Whether he shifted his focus because he wanted to or because Lyft forced him to isn't important.

What matters is that he listened to the market and he adapted.

Despite the increased demand for connectedness and personalized experiences from all donors, today's nonprofits are handcuffed to outdated fundraising models that reserve meaningful engagements for only a select few major donors. Like an elite black car service, high-touch experiences are only offered to those who can afford to pay.

Top donors receive white glove treatment. The major donor team knows their family, their friends, their passions, and even where they like to eat on a Friday night. A good major donor rep builds a real relationship with their donors. And based on that deep knowledge, the rep can tailor communication to the needs of each person.

This model works great for the select few. They feel known and respected, and this personalized experience encourages them to donate where they feel appreciated. It's why major donor fundraising continues to flourish.

But what about the rest?

Well, most nonprofits rely on generic, mass-marketing tactics to reach the bulk of their donorbase. Unfortunately, instead of activating and engaging a wider audience, these tactics are pushing more and more individual donors away. While the top 100 donors enjoy a real relationship, the next 10,000 donors receive a generic institutional letter every month or an email that provides the exact same information they got last year. Zero personalization, zero relationship, zero encouragement to continue their commitment to that nonprofit.

Each year, nonprofits ignore the essential changes in our new reality. They alienate the thousands of rank and file individuals passionate about the cause. They're focusing on the black car service while innovative platforms like GoFundMe or TOMS shoes provide for-profit alternatives for smaller donors to feel like they are having a direct impact on the world. And they're doing it with cutting-edge technology that is available to everyone — even small nonprofits.

THE FUTURE OF GIVING

During previous periods of technological innovation, nonprofits could wait to adopt a new system or software until it was well established. On some level, donors once understood how hard it was for nonprofits to buy and adopt the newest technologies to upgrade their experiences. Not anymore. It's time for nonprofits to stop ignoring change and start embracing it.

Today, powerful tools that create personalized experiences are everywhere. They are more accessible and affordable than ever. For every unattainable giant in software, there are two or three affordable competitors. Nonprofits are out of excuses for ignoring our new connected, hyper-personalized realities. And impersonal direct response marketing has become intolerable for today's donor.

The longer you wait to tailor your marketing and fundraising tactics to the interests and goals of your everyday donor, the less they will trust you, the less effective your strategies become, and the less secure your future as an organization will be.

The days of disconnected, impersonal fundraising are gone. It's time to be responsive to every donor's needs.

CHAPTER 2:

THE NEW DONOR EXPERIENCE

"A relationship is not a fixed state; it's an ever-growing and deepening reality based on mutual openness and on a shared willingness to follow mutual passions. It's a beginning, not an ending."

– Jennifer McCrea and Jeffrey C. Walker,
The Generosity Network

In the 1940s and '50s, several innovative nonprofits discovered the key to successfully scaling their fundraising efforts. They tapped into shared experiences and met their audience where they were: at home. They sent direct mail to people's houses, hosted telethons on TV and radio, and took out print ads in the daily newspaper that appeared on everyone's driveway each morning.

These traditional broadcast tactics were fundamentally successful because this was how communication worked: mass media was everywhere.

Everyone watched live viewings of *American Bandstand* and read the same front-page story in the local newspaper. Nonprofits could reach a wide audience with a single message because they knew everyone was consuming that message the same way.

Suddenly more aware of different needs across the globe, the average donor in Lincoln, Nebraska could now contribute to those causes through direct response. They mailed in their $50 contribution, and could feel a sense of generosity and warmth for supporting a good cause. And when the next call for support arrived in the mail, or by phone, or via television, they would respond again.

These models thrived for the next fifty years because mass media was the only media. Consumers weren't presented with any alternatives. They couldn't turn off the TV to watch a show on their computer, and they couldn't halt their newspaper subscription and scroll through multiple online news outlets for other stories on their phone. And they certainly couldn't conduct their own research on the internet and find nonprofits making a difference in a cause that mattered to them.

And then the internet arrived, and everything began to change.

THE LACK OF EVOLUTION IN NONPROFIT FUNDRAISING

As the internet evolved in the late 1990s and nonprofits started the move to "digital" fundraising, they only marginally modified their old push-based, direct response tactics to work in a digital world. Monthly direct mail appeals were simply repurposed as email appeals, donor brochures were translated into websites, and radio broadcasts were made available online. The internet was nothing more than a digital replica of traditional fundraising models from the past forty years.

A BRIEF HISTORY OF FUNDRAISING		
PRE-1950 **COMMUNITY ORGANIZED**	**1950S** **DIRECT RESPONSE**	**EARLY 2000s** **ONLINE FUNDRAISING**
• Localized • Self-organized • Collaborative • Personal action • Door-to-door • Small meetings • Canvasing	• National • Industrial • Undifferentiated • CPR/RFM • Mass mailings • Telefundraising • TV ads	• Internet • DRF. but online • Impersonal • CPC/CTR • Email blasts • Display ads • Social noise

Fundraising tactics from the past evolved with new mediums, but centered around push tactics designed to steal attention and expand reach. What we know now is that is unsustainable for the future of fundraising.

Before our new connected age, push-based, direct response tactics were tolerable. They represented the only means available to many nonprofits to connect with a broad audience. Generic direct mail acquisitions or telethons might yield a small response rate, but the lifetime value of the new donors justified the expense. Plus, what else could they do?

Following the advent of more personalized digital experiences and the democratization of information on the internet in the mid-2000s, typical response rates started to shrink. And, more importantly, donor retention suffered and donors began to feel alienated by the barrage of institutional, impersonal, broadcast communication.

By 2008, the release of the iPhone, Facebook, and Twitter helped to put a nail in the coffin of broadcast-style fundraising. Response and retention rates have dropped and leading nonprofits have realized that they can no longer hound donors with the same messages and hope for a better response. Yet, amidst the decline of traditional newspapers, broadcast television, and other mass media, one-to-many models, many nonprofits still hold tight to their traditional way of fundraising.

THE VANISHING SHARED BROADCAST EXPERIENCE

The internet has always been a competitive environment, but over the last fifteen years, that competition has exponentially increased. These days, companies, content-creators, and our personal network of friends and family all compete for our attention. Personalized streaming services and curated social media feeds have risen in prominence thanks to nearly-ubiquitous internet access. For anyone competing for attention in this new curated world, the solution is to stop adding to the noise and start serving up only what audiences actually want. How do you know what people want? Pay attention.

Algorithms collect new data points every time we like, share, block, and scroll. The behavioral-based algorithms teach these platforms to adapt to this data and design a curated feed of all the things we love in real-time. As a result, our universal experiences are shared between fewer and fewer individuals. We no longer tune in to the news cycle via nightly network news, or patiently wait for the next episode of *Seinfeld* on Thursday nights.

In its place, we have smaller communities filled with more passionate, like-minded people. We share particular interests, preferences, and community with people whose hyper-connected, curated worlds look like ours. We not only choose our entertainment but we also choose when we will consume it. We create social media groups and group texts to keep in touch with the community we truly care about, and we share the information that matters most to us with them. We don't follow news outlets, we custom design our news to give us updates on the topics we actually care about, and anything that falls outside of our spheres of interest typically remains out of sight and out of mind.

That doesn't mean that we've stopped caring. We've just started to care in different ways than we did in the past. In fact, Millennials, as digital natives, tend to care more about the specific things that enter their world. As noted in *The Washington Post*, "While previously generations may have been motivated to volunteer by their companies, Millennials are much more likely to be influenced by their peers than by their supervisors, 65 percent to 44 percent. And only 11% had their donation deducted from their paycheck, a method that for older generations was often considered the standard way to give at the office."[7]

This shift in the way we consume and engage with the world has also extended to our sense of generosity. The causes we care about become part of our curated experience. This, in turn, has had a profound impact on the relationship between the donor and the nonprofit. Fundamentally, this vanishing shared narrative means that nonprofits can no longer depend on generic, one-size-fits-all

---

7   Brigid Schulte. "Millennials are actually more generous than anybody realizes," The Washington Post, June 24, 2015, https://www. washingtonpost.com/news/wonk/wp/2015/06/24/millennials-are-actually-more-generous-than-anybody-realizes/

communication strategies. Instead, donors expect the nonprofits they support to understand them, and to help them design their own donor experience, just like the for-profit brands already do.

Instead of balking in the face of these changes, nonprofits should be embracing them whole-heartedly. Because the truth is the new hyper-connected reality is primed to create opportunities for people to support causes.

The for-profit world has already recognized a way to leverage this opportunity, introducing a new competition for fundraisers: cause marketing.

THE NEW COMPETITION: CAUSE MARKETING

Cause marketing is a way of capitalizing on our desire to support — and actually be a part of — movements that matter deeply to us via brands we trust. The idea behind cause marketing is simple: demonstrate that the brand is doing more than just making a profit and show how customer participation supports a good cause. This has a broad appeal to both those who care about the cause and brand-loyal customers. The communities already invested in a particular cause now have a reason to shop the company's products. Meanwhile, loyal customers can feel bolstered by the fact that they are affecting change through their buying decisions.

Back in 2016, Patagonia created a campaign that allowed Black Friday shoppers to help the planet while buying holiday presents. The company announced that they would give 100% of sales generated on the popular shopping holiday to support grassroots organizations working to protect the air, water, and soil.

To help support the planet, customers just needed to make a purchase at one of Patagonia's many stores on Black Friday. Both loyal customers and first-time buyers rallied around the campaign, excited by the convergence of relevant engagement (Black Friday) and instant gratification. By the end of the day, Patagonia raised $10 million in sales.[8]

Nonprofits already act as a connection between donors and the causes they care about most. What they currently lack, and what brands like Patagonia who invest in cause marketing understand, are the strategies to make those causes relevant and timely to donors. For-profit companies appeal to customers who are already building communities and conversations around the cause and turn them into loyal consumers. They work to introduce their brand in those spaces, create opportunities to involve their audience in the work they're doing, and elevate them from customers to agents of change.

The secret is to understand the audience, their motivations and values, and then interact with them in a personalized way. Take for example Sand Cloud Towels. Sand Cloud Towels is an ecommerce site that sells Turkish beach towels from their office in San Diego, California. Through detailed reports and daily interactions with their ideal customers, they started to understand who their audience was, and more importantly, what they cared about. In this case, the customers were deeply connected to the beach communities and wanted to protect and care for shorelines around the world.

---

8   Parija Kavilanz. "Patagonia's Black Friday sales hit $10 million — and will donate it all," CNN, November 29, 2016. https://money.cnn.com/2016/11/29/technology/patagonia-black-friday-donation-10-million/index.html

So, Sand Cloud Towels used their brand to champion and affect positive change around beach preservation. It was a natural fit for their product and for their company, which was made up of a group of passionate Southern California natives. The combination of a high-quality product and growing community of activated customers excited about the opportunity to create real change resulted in fast, meaningful growth.

Soon, they expanded their online community into an offline experience. Sand Cloud Towels hosted community beach cleanups and highlighted participants on social media. They encouraged their customers to host their own beach cleanups, creating communities around the cause. Their customers became the face of the movement, and in the end, solidified their brand.

While Sand Cloud Towels is not a household name, they have created a motivated and loyal community. They've harnessed the power of shared experiences and common goals and brought it to their customers. Their small community is full of excited advocates that bring in new like-minded individuals every day, both online and on the beach.

The Sand Cloud Towels and Patagonia examples show us that marketers are leveraging customers' core motivations to do the things that nonprofits have traditionally been best at: changing the world for good. The bad news is that, right now, they're seeing more success than many traditional nonprofits. But the good news is that they're not doing anything that nonprofits can't.

NEW DONOR EXPECTATIONS

Today's donors want to feel appreciated and heard — and they want to feel a connection to your cause on their terms, but especially during the times that they're most interested. They don't want to wait for your schedule to hear updates or learn more about programs they're invested in. In fact, 63 percent of customers are highly annoyed by the way brands continue to rely on the old-fashioned strategy of blasting generic ad messages repeatedly, according to Marketo.[9] And this statistic makes sense when you think about the ways in which we interact in our hyper-connected world. Instant gratification and gamification are at the heart of all our experiences.

Social media apps refresh as you scroll, giving you more of what you want with virtually no wait time. Online retailers offer faster shipping with better tracking information. Fitness trackers will remind you to move every twenty minutes and celebrate every time you surpass 10,000 steps. Even when you're trying to remove yourself from the endless scroll of updates, smartphones will send congratulatory notifications for your restricted screen time. Whether we like it or not, we are all primed to receive real-time feedback and be rewarded for our actions.

On top of that, we are living in a world of 24-hour news cycles. Each of us is inundated with new disasters, causes, and crises to care about every single day. The result is a deep, constant desire to help

---

9 "Consumers to Brands: The Louder You Scream, the Less We Care," Marketo, June 22, 2019. https://www.marketo.com/newsroom/press-releases/2015-06-22-Consumers-to-Brands-The-Louder-You-Scream-the-Less-We-Care/

and an unconscious need to see impact immediately. Nonprofits who respond to this perfect storm in a way that is relevant to their donors will succeed.

New Epsilon research indicates 80 percent of consumers are more likely to make a purchase when brands offer personalized experiences. Kevin Mabley, SVP Strategy and Analytics, told Epsilon:

> *Digital transformation is no longer optional. It is required for brands to improve customer experiences and remain competitive. The research findings are further evidence that bringing together customer intelligence and customer experience to drive personalization has a direct impact on a brand's bottom line. Yet, many brands are still lacking the end-to-end digital maturity required to be successful, including a customer-centric organizational structure, connected and integrated marketing technology and actionable data-driven insights.*[10]

Unfortunately, most nonprofits are stuck using models that make it almost impossible to respond to donors personally at scale and move away from traditional broadcast-style experiences. The result is underserved donors who aren't inspired to give because they can't find an organization as passionate as they are.

---

10   "New Epsilon research indicates 80% of consumers are more likely to make a purchase when brands offer personalized experiences," Epsilon, January 9, 2018. https://us.epsilon.com/pressroom/new-epsilon-research-indicates-80-of-consumers-are-more-likely-to-make-a-purchase-when-brands-offer-personalized-experiences

THE MAGNIFIED IMPORTANCE OF AUTHENTICITY AND TRUST IN FUNDRAISING

Trust, transparency and hyper-relevant communication are even more important to nonprofit donors than the average consumer of a product. Choosing a charitable cause is often a much more personal decision than buying a new rain jacket or beach towel. Indeed, charitable giving is more often than not born from a strong, personal motivation.

A couple unable to have their own kids instead sponsors children in Uganda and India. A mother uses charitable giving to introduce her children to social issues and promote global citizenship. A son who lost his dad to a rare cancer now fundraises for a charity that supports early detection programs. A Vietnam War veteran knows the hardship of reintegration after deployment and supports three organizations working to fill this gap for younger men and women returning from active duty.

Giving is massively personal, yet charitable organizations are losing individual donors because they are unable to provide the personal connection that today's donors have come to expect from their favorite brands. In order to compete in the age of digital distraction, nonprofits must start leveraging more responsive fundraising tactics to tap into the population's already-present desire to affect positive change.

As Jeremy Beer says in *The Forgotten Foundations of Fundraising*, "Weaker, transactional relationships are characteristic of the least successful organizations. Stronger, relational connections characterize the most successful organizations. Or, to borrow from the Dutch priest and theologian, Henri Nouwen, we misserve our donors if we 'have not given them an opportunity to participate in the spirit of what we are about. We may have completed a successful transaction, but we have not entered into a successful relationship.'"

THE SOLUTION IS RESPONSIVE FUNDRAISING

Responsive fundraising puts the donor at the center of fundraising and grows giving by personalizing each donor's journey. It responds in real time to the needs of each individual. The responsive approach builds trust and invites people to move closer to the cause through authentic engagement. It replaces mass messaging and direct response with one-to-one, relationship building at scale.

Responsive fundraising considers the preferred communication channel of each individual when highlighting their contribution. It makes it easy for donors to share the ways they've made a positive impact on the world. It gives them information to pass along to their inner circles and show new potential donors that they can use social influence in addition to financial contributions to move the cause forward. Responsive fundraising listens for donor signals to better understand each individual's passions and engagement with the cause. And a responsive fundraising model creates new ways to show gratitude and give back to their donors at every opportunity.

Responsive fundraising forgoes traditional approaches that focus on organizational needs and convincing donors to respond a certain way. Instead, responsive fundraising **listens** to donors in order to understand intent and desire. It **connects** with donors personally and **suggests** best- fit actions that deepen their engagement.

Responsive fundraisers stand shoulder-to-shoulder with donors in a united front to move the cause forward. In this new model, nonprofits shine the spotlight on donors, who want and need to feel like they are truly participating in the cause.

It's a fundamental change necessary to build lasting relationships with **all** your donors. It's the way that nonprofits can treat every donor like a major donor.

1MISSION'S RESPONSIVE FUNDRAISING STRATEGY

Nate Hughes leads donor development for 1Mission in Phoenix, AZ. 1Mission partners with families to build houses in Mexico and Central America. 1Mission is committed to several responsive practices but one story about listening to donors really struck me. I'll let Hughes tell the story in his own words:

> Our house-to-house program is our partnership with people in the real estate industry. We partner with primarily real estate agents, but we also serve mortgage lenders and title agents. At this point we've even expanded to include a solar salesman.
>
> The whole program came about in a really organic way. We had a real estate agent who went down to Mexico on one of our construction trips and built a house. When he got home, he called our VP of Operations and said, "Hey. I want to figure out a way to make a bigger difference in our industry. I want to figure out a way to give back."
>
> I met with him, and we embarked on this year-and-a-half long journey — me learning a lot about the real

estate industry, him helping me learn, and both of us working together to craft and create a program. We launched a program the following April that gave real estate agents the opportunity to give a portion of their commission to put a family in a house. Buy a house, give a house. It's the best of all the social marketing world. The program is able to tie two industries together and connect donors directly to their impact.

The most critical choice made by Hughes and the entire 1Mission team was dedicating themselves to an eighteen-month journey with the real estate agent in order to learn more and create a program that made sense to all involved parties. Think about any significant relationship in your life. A marriage does not only exist on the wedding day and every subsequent anniversary. The bond between a mother and her child reaches far beyond each birthday celebration. Long-term, meaningful relationships deepen with each interaction that occurs during everyday life. They flourish in the big moments and the small ones. They strengthen when each side celebrates the other or helps through difficult times. Donor relationships are no different.

To maintain relationships with individual donors, your focus must shift from collecting money to cultivating a relationship. Remove the transactional mindset that says your only focus should be on end-of-year revenue reports. Instead, focus on the individuals who committed themselves to the same cause as you.

Connecting with each person in a contextual way allows you to suggest the right next step, at the right time. Deeper connections lead to expanded generosity and, ultimately help you do more good.

IT'S TIME FOR CHANGE

A good number of nonprofits I speak to are initially resistant to change. When I introduce the concept of responsive fundraising to them, they commonly respond with, "We don't have the resources to create relationships with all our donors."

Historically, this was true. The average Donor Development Officer can realistically only maintain relationships with 100-150 major donors, which means that the vast majority donors receive the exact same communication from the organization. The same mail piece, email, and web experience.

Many organizations I talk to insist that a more personal approach is unrealistic, and besides, "our strategy has always worked in the past." In a sense, they are right. It is unrealistic for your staff to build personal relationships with 10,000-plus individual people, and your current method **did** work in the past. But, like it or not, our world has changed.

Remember, these days donors expect to see their impact immediately, and if they don't, they can move onto another organization, stop giving altogether, or find other outlets to make an impact. The good news is that the reason donors expect what they expect is because it's possible for nonprofits to meet those expectations.

The risk of not adopting a responsive approach to fundraising has become too high. Ignoring what your donors care about, and how they're telling you to communicate with them, is to show them the door. Donors can find personalized experiences everywhere, and they are aware of the number of problems that exist and need help. If you're not being responsive to them, they will move on.

CHAPTER 3:

COLLECTING SIGNALS FROM THE MODERN DONOR

"We have to devise means of making known the facts in such a way as to touch the imagination of the world. The world is not ungenerous, but unimaginative and very busy."

— Eglantyne Jebb, Founder of Save the Children

If you share a Netflix account with family or friends, you might notice that each profile has vastly different suggestions. That's because Netflix bases its suggestions on the interests you've signaled. Netflix is a massive corporation, with millions of users, but its algorithms are always working to segment users by persona built using historical and behavioral data. Netflix knows that not all data is created equally and pulling the most relevant data will illuminate the right user experience, thus creating more loyal customers.

They don't segment by the amount of time you've streamed or the number of months you've been a customer because that doesn't reveal anything about what resonates with you on the platform. Instead, they track affinity and engagement — what kinds of programming you like and how you engage with their platform. Responsive nonprofits are using the same approach to segment their donors by preferences and motivations.

Before you start adapting The Responsive Framework, you need to stop and take inventory of your current donor base. Who are they? What are their interests, passions, likes, dislikes, behaviors, motivations? Where do they live? Who are their friends? How do they communicate with you and others? Getting a strong understanding of who your donors are will equip you with the information you need to start becoming more responsive. That's where donor personas come in.

UNDERSTANDING DONOR PERSONAS

Think about the unique individuals that create your donor base. Each may share a common interest in your cause, but they are all motivated by something different. They prefer different communications, connections, and information. Just as Netflix users cannot be treated the same simply because they use Netflix to stream video, your donors cannot be treated the same simply because they care about your cause. By creating donor personas, you can track like-minded people more efficiently and create comprehensive, targeted strategies for each segment of donors that will push them through the donor journey as quickly and frequently as possible.

Note that donor journey strategies include a plan for first-time givers and recurring donations. As *Nonprofit Quarterly* tells us, "a 10% improvement in attrition can yield up to a 200% increase in projective value, as with lower attrition significantly upgrade their giving."[11] Your donor personas should include information about how to earn the first gift of time or money, and how to retain your donors with relevant information and engagements.

There are many different ways you can group your donors, including age, geographical location, behavior, online interests, and more. To identify the best way to segment your donor base, talk with your team at large about your goals and priorities for the future. Let's say your nonprofit wants to focus on increasing individual donations online over the next three years. Since 2012, online giving has almost doubled, with nonprofits receiving an average of 28 percent more gifts in 2017 than 2016.[12] This data affirms online giving is an area of growth, making this a worthwhile goal. A clear goal makes it easy to find helpful segments for your donors. In this case, you might segment based on highly engaged, somewhat engaged, and not engaged donors. From there, your team might create three different donor journey maps based on how many touchpoints necessary to get each persona to give and what motivations they share.

---

11   Adrian Sargeant, "Donor Retention: What Do We Know & What Can We Do about It?" Nonprofit Quarterly, August 15, 2014. https://nonprofitquarterly.org/donor-retention-nonprofit-donors/

12   Theodore Kinni, "Four Ways Nonprofits Can Increase Their Impact," Insights by Stanford Business, November 1, 2017 https://www.gsb.stanford.edu/insights/four-ways-nonprofits-can-increase-their-impact

Each donor profile in your nonprofit CRM should allow you to quickly access the most important information, including persona, donor journey position, and demographic data. Without easy access, your team will have an incredibly difficult time being responsive to donors' needs.

Personas are effective because they help you imagine these donor groups as real individuals and then ensure each type gets the kind of outreach that would make sense for them. For example, one persona might be: Kelly, the busy mom passionate about foster care and adoption. She would require much different communications and relevant information than James, the social extrovert who values his talent to activate others to give to adoption. A responsive nonprofit has a plan for both Kelly and James.

To build personas, observe the behaviors of your donors and ask yourself questions about why they are responding the way they are. Use the answers to your "whys" to pull insights and uncover the most important motivations. Why someone gives is a much more valuable and sustainable segmentation criteria than how much they give or through which channel. Those are important to start, but to truly be innovative and responsive, push yourself beyond the obvious to meet donors where they are in their hearts, not their hands. Your nonprofit offers a unique mission, program, and fundraising opportunities, and as such, your donor personas will be much different than other nonprofits in your space.

For example, an arts organization might find three distinct donor segments after an investigation into their constituents. They might see one group who gives because they benefit from the organization's programming and exhibits. The second group might signal that they support arts organizations broadly, but don't necessarily have a personal investment in which communities see an improvement. The third group of donors might be connected to the children's programs and feel less passionately about other programs.

These arts donors encompass vastly different personas than those you might see in an international aid organization. There, you may have donors that give because they see it as part of their role as a global citizen or use it as a tool to teach their children about global issues. Others may give based on their faith commitment. Or some donors are motivated to give during times of crisis, like natural disasters or displaced people during conflict, whereas others are more development focused and prefer investing in projects like primary schools or job training initiatives.

For both these example organizations, the way they message each persona would be distinct and the suggestions they present to donors must vary accordingly. It all comes down to listening to your donors' motivations and tailoring your suggestions based on the information you know.

If you're not ready or haven't collected enough information to segment by motivations yet (also called psychographic segmentation), you can start with more general, behavior-based profiles. The three most common behavior-based donors include: The Disconnected Donor, The Hybrid Donor, and The Tech Savvy Donor.

The Disconnected Donor is the person who doesn't seem to respond to digital prompts. They may prefer in-person events or direct mail, rather than emails. On the opposite end of the spectrum, The Tech Savvy Donor thrives on digital communications, and embraces email, social media, and mobile alerts. As you might infer, The Hybrid Donor falls somewhere in the middle, and may prefer different communication channels at different times.

Knowing their channel preferences, you will automatically intuit that The Disconnected Donor needs very different messaging and outreach than The Tech Savvy Donor. Your team must work towards building a relationship with each type of donor while respecting their preferences. This means engaging with The Disconnected Donor at events, or through calls, handwritten cards, etc. Since The Tech Savvy Donor already prefers online connections, your efforts might go towards figuring out how to build a committed relationship to your nonprofit through Twitter, Facebook or other digital channels.

RESPONSIVE PLAY:
BUILD DONOR PERSONAS

Over enough time, you will see themes between individual donors. Those strong themes can be turned into complete donor personas. You'll use these donor personas to create personalized, relevant donor experiences. Here's how to start building the right personas:

Execute

- Segment donors based on motivational behaviors. An easy place to start is by dividing donors by the topics your nonprofit impacts (e.g. Child Sponsorship, Malaria, Reading, etc)

- Use information from tracking pixels and website behavior to understand how they heard about you, what content they've interacted with, and what they've indicated as important information. Use content topic tagging in emails and your website to automatically tag donors based on their interest in the digital content they view.

- Work as a team to create a biography for each donor persona. Focus on their feelings, what motivates them, what influences their decisions, what they care about, how they communicate and connect with their network, and how they share their ideas.

- Identify the messaging that would resonate most with each donor persona. Discuss when they need emotional messaging, informational messaging, messaging directly from beneficiaries, and messaging from the people at your organization.

- Match the messaging with touchpoints that correspond with the donor journey. Assign relevant CTAs for each touchpoint.

- Pull quarterly reports on engagement and conversion metrics based on each donor personas. Identify areas where they are not interacting with your communications strongly, then A/B test new messaging and new CTAs.

- Over time, add new details to each donor persona based on reports, donor calls, donor surveys, and all other signals you collect.

- Leverage learning to inform optimized nurture sequences for each donor persona. Match the right CTA and content to each communication the donor receives in their journey.

CONSIDER THE DONOR JOURNEY

The donor journey is the path each person takes that leads them to their first act of giving and beyond. Similar to life paths, a donor's path is extremely personal, driven by their individual values, passions, and resources *over time*. Each donor's personal motivations and interactions with your nonprofit should lead your organization to be flexible, innovative, and empathetic as to why they eventually decide to give.

The goal of each interaction should be to move an individual to the next action at the most efficient rate. Whether the action is to open an email, share a video, host a peer-to-peer fundraising campaign or simply read about the progress your organization made in the last six months, you should know for sure that that person will want to engage before you make the suggestion. To paraphrase Tim Kachuriak from NextAfter, you're looking for a series of small "yeses" that move constituents deeper in their engagement. In order to win those "yeses", you have to understand their journey. Do you know exactly what each donor will engage with? Can you predict how your donor will feel about your nonprofit after each interaction? How accurate are your donation predictions for every ask? If you don't know the answer, you've got some work to do.

RESPONSIVE PLAY:
TRACK DONOR LIFECYCLE

Donor lifecycles are hard to predict, particularly between generations. The best way to stay connected to your donors is to understand how they behave and engage with your organization over time. Here's how you can begin to track a typical donor's lifecycle.

Execute

- Define the lifecycle or your typical donor within your organization. A good place to start is with five basic stages: Aware, Engaged, 1st Time Donor, 2+ Donations, and Advocate. Many donors will skips steps (e.g. you may have Advocates who never give), but this lifecycle is a good place to start for understanding the progress of financial donors.

- Integrate tracking pixels on your website and utilize trackable URLs with every communication and landing page when possible to collect comprehensive data. Make sure web, email, direct mail, and event engagement all flow back into your donor's profile in your CRM. When designing your typical donor journey, differentiate between digitally engaged and unengaged donors. Use automation to combine digital engagement and giving behavior to automatically move donors through the lifecycle,

- Once a person has engaged or given, automate donor call tasks or emails (sent by a person) to check in with donors in order to prevent lapsing. Listen to their needs and help facilitate the next steps in their journey.

- Automate donor tagging for milestone behaviors such as a second gift, event attendance, P2P fundraising campaign, etc. to measure ongoing engagement on all channels.

- Use donor tags to understand how to move donors from one suggestion to the next faster.

- Use A/B test messaging, email marketing, social media advertisements, and more to prompt stalled donors towards their next best action.

- Once you've optimized your base lifecycle, design more detailed lifecycles for specific persona behaviors. For example, a college student will likely have different optimal behaviors, communication preferences, and timelines than a Baby Boomer.

DONOR JOURNEY MAPS

Once you have your donor base segmented into personas and a better understand of each persona's journey, you can begin crafting donor journey maps. These maps will become a valuable tool for your team and help guide all actions within The Responsive Framework.

Remember, the donor journey map is a strategic plan, but ultimately, it reflects human behavior. It should be research-based, but you should always allow for your own intuition. If you ever have a hard time deciding the best option based on the data you have, ask yourself how you would feel if you were the donor. Leading with an empathetic connection to your donors will rarely steer you wrong.

The easiest way to build a donor journey map is by starting with three to five basic personas. Create a spreadsheet and write your persona names down the right hand column. Then write the basic journey stages across the top (e.g. Aware, Engaged, Donor, Loyal Donor, Advocate). Your journey stages will vary based on your goals and the type of organization you are.

In the Aware stage, people are likely hearing about your organization for the first time. They might see a video about your work or see a fundraiser for a friend's birthday on Facebook with money going to your nonprofit. They're getting a high-level understanding of your work. As you build trust and provide social proof that your organization is trustworthy and proactive, people move towards the Engaged phase of the donor journey. During this phase, they might subscribe to your newsletter, follow your social media profiles or regularly check your blogs. Offline, they also talk to their Facebook friend about the work you do and may investigate some of your most influential existing donors.

With thoughtful, responsive engagements, the potential donor will convert into a Donor. They'll make their first act of giving, whether that includes time, money, social influence, goods or a combination of all four. This phase is the most delicate for your nonprofit. If you don't employ the responsive fundraising techniques correctly here, they will not graduate to a Loyal Donor or an Advocate for your organization. You'll fall into the same trap of one-time donors who never engage with your charity again.

Once you've established your grid, begin identifying content, stories, and gift asks that best fit both the stage and persona of each journey and begin filling in your grid. You'll use some content more than once and that's fine. This simple exercise will help you be more intentional about making sure your journey fits the interests and engagement level of each person.

The Journey Map will be your best starting point as you begin to build out marketing automation workflows to better connect with your constituents. Take a look at the image below for a better understanding of what's possible with a content mapping spreadsheet.[13]

Content Inventory							
Asset Name / Title	Buyers Journey Stage	Content Type / Format	Topic	File Path/Location	Status/Date Last Updated		CTA
Malawi Case Study	Engagement	Case Study	Malaria			1/1/18	$10 Can Buy a Net and Save a Life
Poverty Blog	Ambassador	Blog	Poverty			1/1/18	Share with Your Friends
Concert Video	Awareness	Video	Institutional		To be created		Find Out How We are Eliminating Malaria (site and emailsignup)

Plotting your content marketing in a spreadsheet provides quick visibility into each touchpoint with your donor, including what they think and feel about your organization at that moment.

You'll know you've finished the donor journey map when everyone on your team can quickly understand how your donors feel during each touchpoint. Once you know how they feel, what they are interested in, and what they want to do next, it's easy to improve conversion and loyalty.

With your donor personas and donor journey maps in place, you're ready to jump into the three main steps of The Responsive Framework.

---

13 Download a sample version at https://www.virtuouscrm.com/resources/ tip-sheet/content-mapping-spreadsheet/

RESPONSIVE PLAY:
CREATE DONOR NURTURE SEQUENCES TO REFLECT YOUR DONOR JOURNEY

Nurture sequences are workflows made of the communications and engagements that push donors through the donor journey. Each sequence is tailored to the motivations and values of each donor persona. Because individual donors will move through nurture sequences at different speeds, it's important to automate as much as you can so that no one receives more or less from your nonprofit than what they really want. Here's a way to set your nurture sequences up to run automatically so that you can focus on other tasks.

Execute

- Use your content mapping sheet to identify suggestion and conversion points.

- Write emails with personalization elements to ensure each donor persona receives the content they want in a context they care about.

- Create other creative assets based on each donor persona and what they will find relevant and interesting.

- Test messaging, creative assets, and timing to get an idea of what resonates best with each donor persona.

- Use trackable URLs and tracking pixels on your website to report on traffic, conversions, and donor behavior on landing pages for each persona and content piece.

- Create automation workflows to move donors through nurture sequences of emails, calls, letters, etc. Use donors' digital engagement level determine how frequently you communicate. Donors who engage with email and web more often don't mind more frequent touches, assuming that the communication is relevant and not always asking for a gift.

- Pull monthly reports to understand which suggestions and content in the nurture sequence are converting at the highest rate and how you might optimize them for future donors.

CHAPTER 4:

THE RESPONSIVE FRAMEWORK: AN ADAPTIVE SOLUTION

"It may be true that our work, or our issues, touch everyone. But that doesn't mean they matter to everyone. Relevance is relative, and people are busy. Our work is only relevant when people tell us it is. When they feel connected to it."

— Nina Simon, The Art of Relevance

On October 4, 2009, NFL players stormed football fields across the country ready to shove, tackle, and rush their way to victory — the same way they had every week since 1920. This Sunday was remarkably different, however. Every person on the field, from the referees to the linebackers, wore pink accessories as part of their uniform. An unmistakable addition to the male-dominated world of professional football.

That 2009 season marked the first year of the partnership between the NFL and The American Cancer Society. Since then, every

October to celebrate Breast Cancer Awareness Month, the NFL shows support by wearing pink on the field as well as donating proceeds from certain merchandise sales for new research initiatives. As unexpected as the collaboration may have seemed at the time, it made perfect sense to me.

For decades, breast cancer was seen as primarily a woman's issue. The most famous fundraising event for breast cancer, Susan G. Komen's Race For The Cure, reflected what ACS assumed about their audiences. Crowds of mostly women walked in cities around the country to raise money, find community, and show support for survivors and their families. Komen has been incredibly successful in fighting cancer and rallying local communities. But ACS knew that around 1 percent of all breast cancer cases in the United States occur in men, and that cancer of any kind affects the entire family — not just women. They needed to find a way to invite men to the fight.

The NFL offered the perfect opportunity. Men could cheer for their favorite teams while supporting victims and survivors of breast cancer, often finding support for themselves and their families. With resources and relevant marketing strategies, football fans received information they might have otherwise missed about prevention, care, and advocacy. The partnership not only connected millions more to the cause, but it also raised $15 million in donations from 2009 to 2016.

This wasn't purely a play to men, either. In 2009, nearly a third of NFL fans were women, and today that has grown to nearly half.[14] The alignment with ACS had a powerful influence on the future of NFL, too, by aligning the sports-oriented organization to a charitable cause.

What the American Cancer Society did, without knowing it, was implement The Responsive Framework. Leadership heard the stories of fear and triumph from men and women personally affected by breast cancer, but didn't see the reality reflected in much of the fundraising strategies for breast cancer. ACS identified the disconnect and found a solution that many Americans responded to intensely and immediately.

Suddenly, the stories of entire families were included in the conversation. Their pain and fears were felt by like-minded people. Their celebrations included a broader, more connected community. The suggestion that they be included in Breast Cancer Awareness month created a new sense of commitment and generosity that surpassed all expectations.

Interestingly, in 2017, the NFL followed The Responsive Framework and deepened their partnership with the American Cancer Society. Throughout 2016, defensive end Devon Still publicly waged a war against Stage 4 neuroblastoma on behalf of his daughter Leah. Still received immense support from the public, as well as NFL commissioner Roger Goodell. Not only did the NFL listen,

---

14 Liz Hampton, "Women comprise nearly half of NFL audience, but more wanted," Reuters, February 4, 2017. https://www.reuters.com/article/us-nfl-superbowl-women/women-comprise-nearly-half-of-nfl-audience-but-more-wanted-idUSKBN15J0UY.

but it brought viewers in close by connecting them with real, authentic stories.

Still was thankful for the outpouring of generosity, but hoped to take the commitment from the NFL one step further. He suggested that the organization expand beyond breast cancer during the month of October to other forms of cancer. Goodell and the NFL agreed, and made the changes during the 2017 season.

Still told *Sports Illustrated*, "It lets me know that he's [Goodell] listening. For a long time, we have been supporting causes close to the heads of the NFL. To find out they are really following through with this, it makes it feel like the players are gaining more of a voice."[15]

THE RESPONSIVE FUNDRAISING FRAMEWORK

The Responsive Framework doesn't just result in increased revenue or increased awareness — it improves the quality of the relationship between each individual donor and your organization. It centers the donor in the cause and pulls them closer to the good with

15 Jenny Vrentas, "The NFL Moves On From Pink October," Sports Illustrated, December 13, 2016. https://www.si.com/mmqb/2016/12/13/nfl-breast-cancer-awareness-month-october-becomes-all-cancer-awareness-month

each engagement. Every interaction is deeper and more meaningful because both sides are committed to each other and the cause.

Before your organization adopts The Responsive Framework, you must understand that it is cyclical in nature. Responsive nonprofits commit to a future of experimentation, failure, evolution, and iteration. Being responsive means being curious and proactive on behalf of those who trust you to do good. Where previous fundraising eras required very few major changes, responsive fundraising anticipates fundamental shifts, recognizes the exponential rate at which our connected world is engaging, and prepares for change. Before you start worrying about the major changes your nonprofit will have to implement to become responsive, know that at its core, The Responsive Framework is meant to be simple and straightforward.

The Responsive Framework involves three main actions:

- Listen
- Connect
- Suggest

Although the behavior is unique in each stage, the main driver is the same: to learn more about your constituents and connect with them in the ways that they actually want. Responsive fundraisers model the ways in which a major donor relationship is cultivated. The aim is to always look for clues about what people want to give, why, and how that might change over time.

Following, we'll define each part of the strategy and then outline key plays your nonprofit can execute now to begin implementing the framework.

PART 1: LISTEN

Successful relationships are all built on a foundation of intentional listening. Listening directly combats the problem of fractured attention in today's connected, curated reality.

There was a time, before personalized experiences, when content marketing simply meant saying more. Nonprofits were less focused on relevance, and more on quantity. Marketers needed their brand to be everywhere, all the time. Social media timelines filled with repetitive images and meaningless captions. Blogs regularly transformed a single tweet into 500-word articles. And direct mail programs swelled to eighteen-plus pieces per year. The logic seemed to be, "If we can't be the loudest, we might as well talk the most."

That approach was never sustainable.

Next, the era of quality arrived. Blogs expanded to be 1,200 words. Direct mail campaigns became less frequent with higher production quality. YouTube videos evolved from thirty-second clips to hour-long narratives. Social media feeds switched from chronological order to algorithmic displays, meaning users saw more of what they wanted and less of the noise. Quality started to mean more, but users still felt like they were being talked *at* instead of *with*.

Finally, the magic happened. For-profit brands realized in order to earn the engagement they needed to grow, they had to listen more than they talked. User experiences became paramount. So much so that in April 2019, the cosmetic company Lush, famous for bath bombs and environmentally-responsible products, announced on Instagram, "We are tired of fighting with algorithms, and we do not want to pay to appear in your newsfeed. So we've decided it's time to bid farewell to some of our social channels and open up the conversation between you and us instead."[16] Then, they opened up social discussions between users through a community hashtag, and refocused their customer care team's efforts on responding directly to customers. Lush, and others like them, created revenue, growth, and advocates out of a more personalized experience. They caught on to the trend that 80 percent of consumers are more likely to make a purchase when brands offer personalized experiences.[17]

And it happened to donors too. Ellinger said it perfectly in *The New Nonprofit* when he wrote, "Donors conflate how many times they donate per year and how many times they should be solicited: 'I give every June and December. Save your money and just mail me them.' Or, in other words, fundraisers think you must ask 50 times to get two gifts. Donors think you must ask two times."

---

16 https://www.instagram.com/p/Bv_F76GFOZw/?utm_source=ig_embed&utm_campaign=dlfix

17 "New Epsilon research indicates 80% of consumers are more likely to make a purchase when brands offer personalized experiences," Epsilon, January 9, 2018. https://us.epsilon.com/pressroom/new-epsilon-research-indicates-80-of-consumers-are-more-likely-to-make-a-purchase-when-brands-offer-personalized-experiences

The experiences that lead to consistent, reliable growth begin the moment you listen more than you talk. Responsive fundraisers observe behaviors, solicit feedback, and notice trends in an effort to remain curious about who their donors are and what they care about.

RESPONSIVE PLAY:
QUARTERLY SURVEYS

Donor signals via enriched data is invaluable to understanding who your donor is and what motivates them. It's also just as critical to get direct feedback from your donors through quarterly surveys. Of course, you can send surveys as frequently as you'd like, in fact, some donors might signal they want a more open line of communication. But, only send surveys when you have the bandwidth to execute meaningful action from the results. Donors will feel increasingly frustrated if they tell you what matters to them and you continue to ignore their wishes.

Here is an efficient way to automate a workflow in order to send meaningful quarterly surveys that serve both you and your constituents.

Execute

- Assign donor persona tags to your constituents in order to properly segment them before sending a survey. Remove any donors that have indicated they don't want to connect via email or chat.

- Identify the 4-5 pieces of data you'd like to learn from donors and the questions that will elicit meaningful responses. Stick to "how" and "why" questions rather than either/or questions that don't provide deeper context for your team. Don't assume donors fully understand your cause as you craft your questions.

- Write an email that explains the reason for the survey, the information you're hoping to gather and the ways in which the donors' answers will affect programs and initiatives. Add personalized elements (first name, interests, geolocation, etc.) through your email marketing platform where possible.

- Create tags that automatically identify donors who provide in-depth feedback so your team can follow up with a donor call.

- Work together to pull insights and assign action items to provide a more relevant, meaningful experience to your donors based on the personas of donors who completed the survey.

Definition of Terms

- **Donor Persona** - An ideal donor profile that describes an individual's attributes, including demographic, location, behaviors, habits, interests, needs, and other information. Nonprofits group donors into common personas based on shared attributes. For example, "Ashley the College Student" would represent a subset of donors with shared preferences.

- **Donor Tags** - A value or attribute assigned to a donor record that helps you quickly identify and define groups in your database

RESPONSIVE PLAY:
ENRICH YOUR DATA

Many nonprofits have limited visibility into the types of constituents they have on their file. Without comprehensive access to data, there is no easy way to discover motivations or pull behavior-based insights to inform your responsive fundraising strategies. In order to add context, understand your donors and set yourself up for successful responsive fundraising, start by enriching your data to get to know each donor on a micro level and compare macro trends across donor personas.

Execute

- Use Social Media Scraping in Virtuous to grab the social media profiles for each constituent. Good social scraping includes pictures, employment information and age information for each donor.

- Establish wealth data through a service like DonorSearch to append constituent profiles. Wealth data should include net worth, best gift amount, and basic philanthropic giving/interests outside of your organization.

- Use social media integration to determine Twitter followers for each donor to identify digital influence. Make connections with other donors, the influencers they engage with and the frequency and intensity with which they post online about the causes they care about.

- Use physical addresses to determine the density of donors near each constituent's neighborhood and their giving behaviors.

- Use website and email tracking (through URLs or tracking pixel) to determine each constituent's digital engagement or interest. Content can be tagged with a topic so that you can see which types of projects/content get each person most excited.

- Create marketing automation workflows that tag donors based on their wealth, stage of life, passions, social influence, or local network. Wherever possible, use appended donors to create a donor persona or include that individual in an existing personal profile.

- Adjust communication plan so that each persona gets the right content and call to action on the right channel.

Definition of Terms

- **Social Media Scraping** - The act of pulling relevant information from social media profiles to get a better understanding of who each donor is, the people they are connected to, and the topics they talk about most frequently. Modern software can automatically pull in publicly available social and demographic information using email address, phone number, etc.

- **Social Media Integration -** The act of connecting your suite of software with the various social media platforms in order to pull engagement data in real-time. Social media integration can be used to pull in a Twitter feed, post to Facebook, determine social followership, etc.

- **URL Tracking and UTM Codes -** The practice of adding UTM codes or variables to a website URL. These small chunks of text added to the end of links help gather data about engagement on the macro and individual level. For example, this URL could be used in an email to track donation attribution on your giving page at the campaign level. mynonprofit. org/donate?utm_campaign=malawi-water

- **Tracking Pixel -** A pixel embedded in your website that identifies individual visitors and follows their behavior as they move around your website. Pixels use a website cookie to remember visitors and log their behavior in your CRM. Pixels enable personalization on your website and the kind of hyper-personal ads you see on Facebook and Google.

- **Marketing Automation Workflow -** A set of automatic tasks that are triggered based on specific events (e.g. first gift, event attendance, volunteer milestone, etc). Marketing automation was originally built to automatically start a sequence of emails with scheduled delays in between, but has since expanded to include direct mail, task assignments, data updates, etc.

PART 2: CONNECT

Since 2008, organizations who prioritize meaningful engagements, such as "listening to customer needs and feedback" have continued to be ranked as particularly important when it comes to earning trust.[18] But listening is only the first part for nonprofits. Responsive nonprofits must connect the donor signals with their own work. Connect is where you make your organization relevant to donors. The strategies you create during Connect directly impact the breadth and depth of your relationships, which results in increased generosity and improved retention.

In the American Cancer Society example from the beginning of this chapter, responsive fundraisers looked at hospital rooms across the country. They heard the stories of patients and tracked the

---

18 Matthew Harrington, "Trust and the Art of Listening," Edelman, January 23, 2014. https://www.edelman.com/post/trust-and-the-art-of-listening

donor data. Fundraisers knew men cared deeply about breast cancer research, even if they weren't represented in major fundraising events. That represented the first connect moment.

The second, and possibly more important moment of connection, came when ACS fundraisers decided to meet men in their preferred space: Sunday Night Football. Traditional fundraising tactics might have led the ACS to send a direct mail piece to all their male donors or email female donors encouraging them to bring their male loved ones to upcoming events. But responsive fundraisers at ACS took a proactive approach to connection. They went out of their way to make their cause relevant to an underserved, but very connected, donor base with tremendous results.

Your job is to identify the piece of information or story that is most engaging to your donors and facilitate the connection in the way that is most relevant to them. With a variety of communication channels available to you, the more thoughtful your choices for facilitating connection, the faster your message will cut through any noise.

RESPONSIVE PLAY:
ALL STAFF AUTO-PROMPTED DONOR PHONE CALLS

Even in the age of digital communication, intentional phone conversations between two people are still incredibly important — especially to donors. Unfortunately, with so many daily tasks, nonprofit employees often forgo a phone call for an easier, more time-efficient communication method. In order to ensure that your nonprofit never forgets to call your donors, try automating them.

For your calls that don't include a gift ask, try involving your *entire* staff in this process (not just fundraisers). The organizations that we've worked with that take this approach to connecting with donors have a much healthier culture of generosity. This strategy also helps break down walls between internal teams and helps move donors closer to your cause. We'll talk more about this approach later in the book. For now, here's how you can get started.

Execute

- Create an automation workflow that tags donors on specific milestones. These milestones could be anniversary dates, program progress milestones, birthdays, donation amounts, event attendance, or anything else that is important to your organization.

- Decide on a specific number of daily phone calls that every one of your employees can make in order to improve donor relationships.

- Use the workflow to automatically assign each employee the task of calling individual donors based on how many each person can do per day.

- Create a task to update each donor profile in your CRM with information acquired during calls.

- Let the workflow run indefinitely for all donors.

You would not send a text to your mom to tell her she's going to be a grandmother for the first time. That's a moment best experienced in person. That same sense of context, relevancy, and timing should be applied to cultivating donor relationships, too.

In a way, it's easier to think about listening and responding en masse like ACS did as part of their NFL partnership. But when I talk to nonprofits about responding individually in order to provide a personalized Amazon or Netflix experience, responsiveness seems like too big a task. I understand the challenges of personalized connection, but there is hope. The same tools that empower personalization for your favorite brands are available to your nonprofit. Modern strategies and technology like marketing automation have the ability to multiply the power of your current team. I'll talk more about how to do this effectively internally and externally in Chapter 5.

PART 3: SUGGEST

Following the moment of connection with donors, responsive fundraisers suggest the most meaningful next step for each individual person. Instead of using every engagement as an opportunity to ask all of your donors for the exact same amount of money (signaling to donors that they are little more than an ATM to your organization), responsive fundraisers send suggestions that are relevant to the passions, capacity, and engagement level of each individual.

Some suggestions include a variable financial ask, but a great responsive fundraiser recognizes that people have far more to offer than just what's in their checking account.

In terms of the evolution of consumer behavior, suggestions are close relatives of the hyper-relevant advertisements you see on your social media feeds. Print, television, and radio ads of the past required a broad appeal. Although companies knew general demographic information, they did not have access to granular behavioral data to drive the personalized messaging we've all come to rely on. The result of this new model was reduced spending and fewer wasted resources.

As soon as for-profit companies could transition to personalized digital advertising, spending got tighter, conversion costs went down, and resources were used more appropriately. As much as 63 percent of consumers confirm that they think more positively of a brand when they provide content that is more valuable, interesting or relevant.[19] More favorable perception leads to more trust, better advocates and higher revenue.

Suggestions create the same shift in your nonprofit. You know exactly when to suggest giving of money, time, social sharing, content consumption, or nothing at all. Generosity happens more frequently because each suggestion makes sense in the moment to that specific donor. There is no reason for your donors to say no or ignore your suggestion, because they were primed and ready for the next best action.

---

19   Matthew Harrington, "Trust and the Art of Listening," Edelman, January 23, 2014.https://www.edelman.com/post/trust-and-the-art-of-listening

REPEAT INDEFINITELY

The compounding value of The Responsive Framework occurs after you've completed the cycle with an individual donor a few times. It might take a few weeks to walk through each phase, or it could happen in a matter of hours. The result remains the same: more information leads to better understanding, which leads to more relevant suggestions and, ultimately, increased generosity and donor retention.

And remember, as you Listen, Connect and Suggest, your responsive nonprofit should always be thinking in terms of donor personas and the donor journey. Each aspect of The Responsive Framework should be implemented, tracked, and reported against the donor personas your organization has identified and the donor journey touchpoints you've outlined.

CHAPTER 5:

THE 10 PRINCIPLES OF RESPONSIVE NONPROFITS

"Customers will never love a company until the employees love it first."
— Simon Sinek, Start with Why

Throughout this book, you're seeing examples of responsive organizations in both the nonprofit and for-profit spaces. No two examples look the same. Some are large corporations, some are niche nonprofits focused solely on their most passionate advocates, some are small businesses, and some are among the biggest and most widely recognizable nonprofits in the world.

The reason the examples are so diverse is to show that any nonprofit can implement The Responsive Framework. You can be a responsive organization no matter what your cause is, the size of your organization, or your donor base demographics. These details only inform the way you execute The Responsive Framework, not whether you can.

Before we talk about the "why" and "how" behind each part of The Responsive Framework, I thought it would be helpful to discuss the 10 core principles all responsive nonprofits share. Hopefully, you'll recognize most of these in your organization. If not, use them as a jumping off point to discuss with your team how you can prioritize these principles today. If these principles are at the core of everything you do as an organization, both internally and externally, The Responsive Framework will feel like second nature.

1. BUILD RELATIONSHIPS WITH ALL DONORS

A few years back, Jaimie Trussell started as the new Chief Donation Officer at Adult & Teen Challenge USA, a Christian nonprofit that provides addiction relief to teens and adults. On her first day in the office, she celebrated her new position by making a donation on the organization's website. Within minutes, she had an email in her inbox from one of her new coworkers personally thanking her for her generous contribution.

Touched by the thoughtful email, Jaimie left her office and walked down the hall to thank her coworker for the note. "Wow," she said, "You were so quick to respond to my donation!"

Surprised, the woman stared at her blankly and said, "What donation?"

In that moment, the efficiency of their marketing automation process was revealed to everyone. The organization automated their gratitude process in such a way that their thank you emails felt incredibly personalized, authentic, and timely. Even their own CDO had been convinced that the note was typed in real time by her coworker.

The first principle of responsive nonprofits is that they build relationships with all of their donors, not just some. With intentional, strategic messaging, authentic gratitude, and marketing automation, Adult & Teen Challenge employees are able to cultivate lasting relationships with every single donor while also completing their other responsibilities. Without this process, the thank you letter might never have come — a bad impression to leave on the new CDO who is acting in good faith and camaraderie.

When a responsive nonprofit takes the time to map the donor journey, craft personalized messaging around each, and build the infrastructure to engage at the right time with each person, they signal to every one of their constituents that they are a critical part of the organization. It doesn't matter if someone gives $100 or $1,000, no act of generosity is ignored.

It might seem like building a responsive relationship with all donors is impossible, but consider what strong relationships require. Open communication, personalized responses to signals, and support of the other person's passions. You're already doing these things to cultivate lasting relationships with a small subset of donors. Now, you have to democratize those strategies and expand them to your entire donor base using resources, data and software tools available to you in today's hyper-connected world.

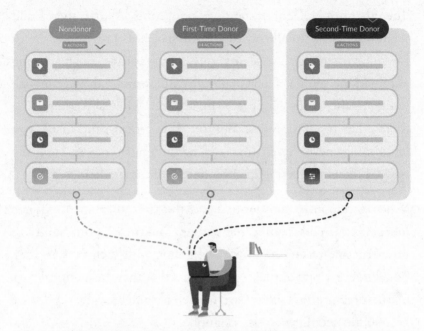

With responsive fundraising and powerful tools like marketing automation, your team will always have a powerful way to engage with your donors.

2. EMBRACE INNOVATION, EXPERIMENTATION, AND FAILURE

There's a phrase you might have heard before: "You don't get fired for choosing IBM." In short, it means that people tend to make the safe choice to avoid putting their own success on the line. They'd rather maintain the status quo than risk failure. In a vacuum, this might be the right approach. But donors do not exist in a vacuum. They're benefiting from the innovation, experimentation, and failure of every brand they know. By trying to avoid failing campaigns or projects, you're actually failing donors.

Innovation and experimentation are the cornerstones of success. Responsive nonprofits are constantly innovating, experimenting, and adapting their processes. They try new things. They embrace new ideas. And they get comfortable with failing.

We are well into the 21st century. Technology is ubiquitous. The software and platforms needed to manage your data and automate your processes are available to you now. The small investment up front results in exponential growth and better donor relationships, which more than validates the purchase.

But you have to embrace the technology and processes whole-heartedly. Teach your coworkers that failure is an opportunity to learn and shouldn't be feared. Encourage smart, creative brainstorming based on the data you collect from your donors. Resist the urge to default to what's comfortable, especially when it compromises your donors' experience of the cause.

Try again. Try something new. Evaluate failure and adopt a new approach. The more flexible and adaptable you are to change, the more exponential your growth will be.

Additionally, know that the severity of failure is drastically reduced when you use The Responsive Framework because you are connecting to and learning new insights from your donors at all times. Every time you send an email, earn a social share, or make a phone call, you're collecting data and responding to it.

By constantly analyzing this data, every idea you pitch will be based in facts and insights from real donors. Yes, you might fail sometimes, but if you're open and communicative with your donor base, you'll have a strong enough relationship to bounce back from any failure and move forward with greater confidence.

My friend Jon Burgess embodied this idea when he spent time leading innovative projects at Compassion International and David C Cook. While at David C Cook, Jon started an Innovation Lab designed to facilitate brave, new ideas. He described his efforts as a way to "create a culture where it's okay to fail". He went so far as to throw parties when an idea failed.

In one of our conversations, Jon said, "We like to reward people whose ideas don't see the light of day. We like to give them gift cards and give them the notoriety. We say, look, it's the process that's as important as anything else. Not the fact that you came up with the winning idea. We'll get to the winning ideas, but we want to reward you for coming in and doing things the right way."

The result of Jon's commitment to innovation was a culture where employees weren't afraid to take risks or dream big. This mentality allowed Jon's team at Compassion to create an immersive international experience where they transform two semi trucks into a working model of their work in India and Uganda. Visitors could walk around, hearing the sounds, seeing the visuals and listening to the stories of the locals who were affected by the work the donors made possible. The 18 wheelers created a microenvironment in order to bring people closer to their cause. The initiative has been incredibly successful and could have never been accomplished if Compassion employees weren't empowered to push beyond what's always been done.

Outlandish decisions for the sake of shaking things up almost never do well. But unique ideas born from reason and insights often do. If your donors trust your intention, then even if your experiments seem unconventional, they will see your vision — and believe in it.

3. FOCUS ON EARNING TRUST

Every relationship thrives on trust and accountability. We all want to know the people we are supporting will do what they say and act in the ways we expect. Unfortunately, over the years, some nonprofits have taken advantage of donors' trust by mismanaging funds and making misguided decisions. Some organizations have recovered from those missteps, some have not.

Likely, you won't need to plan for the biggest blunders. But, you aren't immune to small mistakes or incorrect assessments and judgements. None of us are. The only way to transform those mistakes into learning opportunities rather than letting them ruin all credibility, is to work every day to earn the trust of all your donors.

Own the mistakes that happen while you try to build better donor experiences and do more good in the world. Instead of hiding from these failures, communicate what went wrong with your donors and share how your nonprofit is taking steps to avoid it happening again in the future. You'd be surprised what the accountability will do for your relationship.

Chris Horst and Peter Greer have done an amazing job at building this kind of culture at Hope International. Like every nonprofit, Hope International experiences successes and failures as they try to create good in the world. The difference is that their team admits failure early and often. Chris Horst will actively call donors when a project goes poorly. As counterintuitive as this approach sounds, Hope International has been able to build unflappable trust with their donors, while bringing them closer to the cause. The result has been more sustainable and healthy generosity.

That said, you don't have to wait for something to go wrong to build trust into your donor relationships. Cultivating trust is something you can do every day. Show that you're listening to your donors, reacting to and anticipating their needs. Condition them to expect honesty and accountability, and more importantly, prove that you have all of their best interests at heart. Show that you are someone they can count on, even if you disappoint them every once in a while.

By proactively showing that you listen to donors and genuinely care about their relationship to the cause, you make them more inclined to stay loyal through the challenges you face. They know that in the course of a few decades, the accomplishments and impact you help them achieve will far outnumber the small missteps.

4. UNDERSTAND GENEROSITY IS SOCIAL AND INDIVIDUAL

One of the most heartwarming Twitter accounts out there is @WeRateDogs (and I'm not just saying that as a dog lover). Founded by college student Matt Nelson in 2015, the account, which shares pictures of dogs and offers humorous commentary, has amassed over 8.4 million followers.

What started as a fun parody account has since grown into a sprawling international community united by love for man's best friend. In recent years, Nelson expanded the lighthearted content. Each week, the account shares a different GoFundMe account aimed towards dog care. Some accounts are for individual dogs who require expensive surgery while some raise donations for various shelters and hospitals.

And each week, without fail, the fundraising goals for each campaign are met in under twenty-four hours.

Generosity is an emotional act, propelled by a particular feeling that inspires donors to give. Donors respond to moments of compassion, whether those are driven by grief over a friend suffering through cancer, motivation during a political speech, or even joy in helping a puppy recover from an accident.

But generosity is also social, born out of communities that form around specific causes and passions. That's why responsive fundraising isn't limited by connecting only to individuals in the database. Instead, responsive nonprofits activate the communities of those who are already engaged in the cause.

Nelson built a community of people who are passionate about dogs, and then funnelled that passion into raising money for good causes. You can do the same thing by leveraging your donors' social networks and getting them involved in your cause. Through social media, peer-to-peer fundraising, local events, church, and more, you can begin to integrate into your donors' existing communities and extend an invitation for them to join yours.

Through Listen and Connect, you'll be able to identify the exact right time to suggest new generosity opportunities for donors. Perhaps you'll see an opening to highlight a donor and their story through a series of blog posts, social media videos, and newsletters. Or you might uncover an opportunity to suggest a specific group of donors host events that bring their friends into your nonprofit community. When donors have the chance to signal their participation, they boost their own social currency, feel more connected to your cause and more loyal to your initiatives in the future.

On the other hand, you can also build a new program or community around your cause by seeking out interested donors and creating opportunities for them to connect with each other and your organization.

For example, using geo-location tagging, you might notice a high concentration of donors in downtown Des Moines. You can focus your efforts there, work to figure out what's happening, and create opportunities for a community to form around your cause.

Maybe you host an open dinner in the city to share what's going on with your organization. You invite your Des Moines donors, and encourage them to bring friends. People who don't know each other, but live close to each other, can connect at the event. They recognize a shared interest, and can create new opportunities for community growth and grassroots initiatives on your behalf.

Scott Harrison is notorious for activating communities through his nonprofit, charity:water. On his thirty-first birthday, Scott decided to throw a party and charge $20 at the door to fund water projects. He rallied the local community to supply the drinks and venue. And with that, charity:water was born. Scott's organization has maintained this ethos by staying on the cutting edge of peer-to-peer fundraising. charity:water supporters are empowered to initiate creative fundraising events on behalf of the organizations. The donors throw parties, run lemonade stands or even give up their wedding gifts to fund clean water. Rather than trying to force specific charity:water campaigns on donors, charity:water actively celebrates the creativity of donors in their local community.

Responsive nonprofits take themselves out of the spotlight and highlight the cause and the donor instead. Shift your focus to be community-driven. Create content that donors can share with their social circles. Seek communities that have formed around the cause or go out and build those communities yourself.

5. CREATE GOOD BY BREAKING DOWN SILOS

In a world of shared information and multi-device connections, it's impossible to control how donors come to and experience your nonprofit. They'll hear about you from friends, do their own research online, and see multiple communications from you before you even know their name.

To ensure quality and consistency for all donors, your internal teams need to collaborate more. Silos between programs, fundraising, and communications departments no longer serve your organization, donors, or beneficiaries. The more crossover between teams, and even donors, the more responsive your organization can be.

Whether someone works for the organization, donates, volunteers, or is a beneficiary of the organization, they all have a stake and interest in the cause. Your job is to connect these people, bring them together, and motivate them towards that common goal.

This also means working to bridge the gap between the donors and the beneficiaries. There are plenty of ways you can do this. Maybe you host a lecture by the researcher your nonprofit benefits so donors have the chance to listen to and ask questions of the beneficiaries directly. You can also host volunteer opportunities, send updates from the child or animal the donor is sponsoring, or even organize webinars and digital Q&As that connect field workers with donors. With modern technology there's no longer an excuse for keeping donors at an arm's length from your impact. Close the loop even further, and let members of your organization share their personal stories of connection with the cause.

Everyone wants the same thing — to make a positive impact on the world. All you have to do is give them the opportunity to collaborate towards that common goal.

6. CONTINUOUSLY ADAPT TO NEW BEHAVIORS

Since its inception in 1985, Relay for Life has been The American Cancer Society's most successful fundraising event of all time. The race is held in communities across the country each year, and the organization always sees a spike in giving around each event.

ACS could have been content knowing that this event worked for them, and simply focused on hosting more and more similar events, trying to repeat the success. But instead, they got innovative.

They introduced the Relay for Life mobile app to help individual fundraisers accept and manage donations around the event. Then, they focused on optimizing the app's messaging. They started sending push notifications around timely events and particular user flows to thank donors and share how their contributions were being used. For example, on National Cancer Survivors Day, volunteer fundraisers who had raised over $100 received a notification explaining how this money could pay for one night in a "Hope Lodge" for a patient in need of care. As a result of these timely, personalized messages, in-app giving increased by an estimated 34 percent.[20]

Responsiveness is an ongoing process with no finish line. You have to get comfortable with the idea that you'll never be done and commit yourself to adapting to new behaviors, experimenting and innovating, over and over again.

If you adopt The Responsive Framework, you have to fight back against stagnation. If, through Listen, Connect, and Suggest you find something new that works, you aren't done. You can't default to repeating that success over and over again.

True responsive nonprofits keep changing, innovating, and adjusting. They are always looking to the future. As you well know, technology is changing at an exponential rate. If you're not prepared for the changes coming five, ten, fifteen years down the line, you'll fall further and further behind.

Nonprofits are facing today's generosity crisis because they reacted to change slowly, instead of preparing for it early. The only solution is to dedicate yourself to change. If something is working, look for ways to build on it. If it stops working, come up with a new plan. If it's a tremendous success, identify how to expand it to reach more donors.

This doesn't mean making drastic changes just for the sake of being innovative. Organizations still need to be incredibly thoughtful

---

20 Kelsey Cottingham, "The Impact Of Making An Impact: How The American Cancer Society Uses Personalized Push Notifications To Drive Engagement," Braze Perspectives, September 25, 2018. https://www.braze.com/perspectives/article/american-cancer-society

about the changes they make. Take the responsive view. Listen to your donors, connect with them, and then continually make adjustments informed by what you learn.

7. SAY THANK YOU THREE TIMES FOR EVERY ASK OF GENEROSITY

The funniest moment in a new parent's life is when your child begins mimicking your behavior. Whether it's waving back when you say hello or repeating that curse word you hoped they wouldn't hear, humans mirror behavior from a very early age. That mirroring doesn't stop as we age. In fact, though we become more aware of how others influence our behaviors and actions, that doesn't stop their influence from being effective.

Knowing this, responsive nonprofits model the same generous behavior they're asking from their donors.

There's a saying I love to repeat to my team: generosity begets generosity. This means giving back to your donors even more than they give to you — prioritizing your relationship over their money.

Unfortunately, many nonprofits treat their donors like an ATMs, but those same organizations are finding that the account is dwindling. Responsive organizations, however, work to provide highly meaningful experiences *before* donors give. Never lose sight of the sacrifices your donors are making with their time and money. Put your gratitude for them first, and engage with your donors without planning to ask for money. Once you begin engaging with donors in this way, you'll be able to give them something valuable in return — an emotional experience.

We all have that one friend or family member who only reaches out when they need something. They never call just to catch up. They rarely show interest in your life unless it somehow benefits them. And when they do connect, you know the pretense is just a way to make the ask. It's obvious.

Sound familiar? Nonprofits should avoid appearing this way to their donors. Sometimes, you just have to call to catch up, ask questions about their lives, even give them valuable or relevant information they didn't know they needed. That's how you would treat your major donors, right? Because it works.

To do this at scale for all your donors, you can automate these engagements, creating emails and workflows that trigger automatically to share this messaging with your audience. You don't have to handwrite 1,000 notes every day, but you do have to dedicate yourself to giving more than you are asking if you want the relationship to grow.

Remember, you have to be continuously evaluating, innovating, and adjusting those processes. The flows may be automated, but the content and thought you put into them should always be considerate and personalized.

8. VALUE MOTIVATIONAL INSIGHTS OVER BEHAVIORAL ONES

Communication is a series of signals and responses. Sometimes these signals are verbal, but sometimes they're physical, behavioral, or even unconscious.

For example, let's say you go to coffee with a friend and catch up on her life. She begins to tell you about the stress at her job, and you notice from physical signals that she's tired and feeling defeated. Maybe there are circles under her eyes or her shoulders are slumping. She orders a coffee but doesn't even drink it.

All of these are signals, and once you pick up on them, you know to respond with comforting words, maybe a hug or an offer to help. Throughout this short, seemingly simple exchange, you've displayed a level of emotional intelligence that informed your actions.

Organizations require a strong level of emotional intelligence in order to be responsive. Knowing how to listen to donor signals, form connections, and make informed suggestions, all requires a mature, analytical ability.

So many nonprofits get caught up with a single behavioral signal — "Did they donate or not?" — that they fail to listen to all the other signals donors are giving. Their analysis is rooted only in dollar amounts and number of clicks, that they ignore everything else.

Responsive nonprofits, however, seek out the motivation behind the behavior first. They don't value what someone is doing as much as why they're doing it. For example, let's say you send your donors a video about a new well your team is building. You aren't interested in how many donors watched the video, but why some clicked play and others didn't. What motivated those who watched and what repelled those who didn't?

Knowing why someone is moved to learn about or support a certain cause is more important than the mere fact that they're donating. Once you know their why, you can tailor all future interactions to them and make appropriate suggestions based on a comprehensive donor journey.

9. BELIEVE GENEROSITY IS NOT TRANSACTIONAL

People give for many reasons. They give out of grief, anger, frustration, love, compassion, the list goes on. The disconnect between a donor and a nonprofit begins when the organization focuses on the act of giving, rather than the human heart at its center.

Don't forget the emotion that sits at the heart of generosity. Responsive nonprofits need to embrace a shift in mindset that moves away from treating generosity as a transaction and instead recognize it for the sacrifice it is. Donors don't get anything in return for their generosity except for a reminder that they did some good. That isn't a substantial enough reason on its own to encourage lifelong generosity in the face of being treated as an ATM.

Whether it's as little as $10 or as monumental as $1 million, the donation is still meaningful to that person. You have to do whatever you can, whenever you can, to create a relationship with your givers and recognize their generosity. Your cause means a lot to them, and you are their biggest, often only, connection to a purpose they care about. Don't take that responsibility lightly.

10. KNOW AMOUNT DOESN'T REFLECT PASSION

Who cares the most about your cause — you or your donor? You may believe that, because you are behind the wheel of a nonprofit dedicated to a particular cause, you represent the highest level of concern for it. You sacrifice your time, effort, maybe even finances to the cause, but that does not mean you have more passion for it than your donors.

You can't take a tone of superiority in fundraising or assume that the strength of the connection your donor has is demonstrated in the amount donated. Someone who is only able to donate $50 a month may be perceived as a low-interest donor, but until you get to know them you won't have a true grasp of their level of concern. That $50 monthly donor may have lost a mother to cancer, and now seeks to scrape by whatever she can to donate to its research. You won't know her level of passion until you connect with her personally.

No matter how much someone donates, at the end of the day every donor is making a sacrifice, and they deserve to be honored for it. Donors deserve a democratic experience. You shouldn't treat donors differently based on the amount they give, and you can't relate the amount to a perceived level of concern.

Here's a challenge that I encourage you to take at your nonprofit. What would change about your fundraising strategy if you assumed that every donor cares more about the cause than you do?

PUT THE 10 PRINCIPLES TO WORK

Now that you know the principles your nonprofit should live in order to be responsive to your donors, let's go deeper into why The Responsive Framework is essential and how to implement it at your organization.

CHAPTER 6:

WHY (AND HOW) YOU MUST LISTEN TO ALL YOUR DONORS

"God gave you two ears and one mouth for a reason."

– My Grandmother (& others)

Growing up, my family captured our treasured moments by snapping photos on rolls of Kodak film. Whether we wanted to commemorate a rare accomplishment or remember a small detail, we collected all of it on gloss 4-by-6-inch photos. Kodak was an American institution, with 90 percent of film in the United States bearing the Kodak logo by 1976.[21] At the time, no one in the world thought that Kodak would ever fall from its perch atop the

---

21 Henry C. Lucas, *The Search for Survival* (Santa Barbara: ABC-CLIO, LLC, 2012), 16.

photography industry, much less get delisted from the New York Stock Exchange entirely.

Unfortunately, it did. The demise of Kodak can be attributed to many things. But the most alarming reason was because Kodak ignored the changing behaviors of their customers in favor of maintaining what they'd always done.

In 1975, Steven Sasson was an electrical engineer at Kodak. Using his imagination and the technology of a cassette tape, Sasson developed the first self-contained digital camera. Early versions of the camera were portable only in the technical sense: they weighed eight pounds. But it was an undeniable step forward in the evolution of photography. Still, the early experiments lacked the usability necessary to be a viable product for Kodak to send to market.

Although executives appreciated Sasson's newest invention, they ordered a stop to further iterations of his digital camera, fearing it would interfere with their film sales. In 1975, digital photography wasn't a viable source of revenue. Innovation could have remained a high priority, internally, but it wasn't. It took Kodak until the 1990s before they announced a ten-year plan to truly begin focusing on digital cameras. By that time, Fuji Film and other competitors had already made digital cameras available to the public.

Because of their decades of tremendous success with film sales, the leadership at Kodak could not imagine a world where film photography wasn't the de-facto standard for everyday photographers. Kodak was the clear market leader in photography, but they weren't tuned into the behaviors or interests of customers, and their inability to listen ruined the company. By the turn of the century, Kodak was in trouble. Film sales were steadily declining year after year and their slow adoption of digital strategies meant they were lagging further and further behind their competitors. In 1999, the first cell phone with an included camera was released. The rest is history.

The lesson nonprofits can learn from Kodak's demise is this: your current position doesn't dictate your future success. The culture of your organization does. Kodak had access to the most comprehensive consumer data. They employed the person who invented the first digital camera. Kodak had the capital, technology, talent, and access to lead the digital photography revolution. But they got in their own way.

If you want to continue to grow as an organization and reach donors in a relevant way that drives generosity, you cannot follow the path of years past. You must adopt the path of the future. You must be responsive to what donors are signaling to you.

THE REAL RISK NONPROFITS FACE

Like Kodak, many nonprofits default to the safe option. It's the choice that has led us to the generosity crisis we are currently facing. Internally, many nonprofit leaders discourage perceived risks in obvious and subtle ways. Teams avoid new ideas or strategies lest they lose their job, or worse, impact fewer beneficiaries. Even those excited by change eventually cave to internal forces that make it easier to "stick with what worked" rather than listening attentively to donors and those they serve.

Right now, internal teams are frustrated, to say the least. Stanford found that most employees of nonprofits agreed that their organization was struggling with each of the seven elements of strategic leadership. They cited 56 percent of people saw struggles with board governance, 52 percent agreed to issues with funding, 50 percent talked about struggling to identify impact evaluation, 38 percent with strategy, 35 percent with organization and talent, 18 percent with mission and 17 percent with insight and courage.[22] Your team is not only feeling the stagnation, but they're starting to react to it.

I am saying this as someone who has worked in and with nonprofits for years. I witnessed this aversion to change firsthand. It is what drove my decision to finally build the necessary software to help equip responsive fundraisers to take the road less traveled.

The ironic part, of course, is that innovative new ideas, campaigns, or fundraising strategies don't have to be risky if you're truly connected to your constituents. Listening to what your donors care about, on the micro and macro levels, illuminates exactly which fundraising strategies will resonate with them. It gives you a path forward as well as the ideas to test and optimize quickly.

Truthfully, the real risk is not necessarily in making change. The imminent risk is in believing you know exactly why today's donors care about your cause and what drives them to action.

In March 2014, Rich Stearns, CEO of World Vision USA, an evangelical relief and development organization, made a landmark announcement. The nonprofit would begin to hire Christians who

---

22 Stanford Survey on Leadership and Management in the Nonprofit Sector," Stanford University, November 2017. http://www.engineofimpact.org/wp-content/uploads/2018/03/Stanford-Survey-v20.Final_.171101.pdf

were in same-sex marriages. Leadership decided the time was right to take the first step towards inclusion. States were reversing same-sex marriage bans one by one, and by early 2015, the Supreme Court would decide that all bans on gay marriage were unconstitutional. Stearn and his colleagues thought they were getting ahead of an obvious trend.

Unfortunately, while they were crafting their plan, no one thought to include donors in the conversation. Many of their most passionate and engaged donors disagreed whole-heartedly with the decision. The backlash was immediate and intense.

Adam Nicholas Phillips, a pastor in Portland, described the tumultuous two-day period for *The Huffington Post*. He wrote, "One of the most disgusting parts of the World Vision fiasco was how many people held poor and hungry kids in great need hostage, because of an HR decision in Federal Way, WA."[23]

In a matter of days, World Vision lost nearly 3,500 child-sponsors, donors who were committed to monthly giving to help struggling kids get the water, nutrition, and opportunities they needed to survive. Others organized to bridge the gap — to no avail. Those 3,500 children still lost their opportunities. And no matter what side of the argument you are on, it's easy to agree that no child should have suffered because of a lack of listening.

While there's no way to predict the future, World Vision certainly would have uncovered a more strategic rollout for their new policies

---

23 Adam Nicholas Phillips, "The Wreckage of World Visions' LGBT Reversal Two Years Later," HuffPost, March 29, 2016. https://www.huffpost.com/entry/the-wreckage-of-world-visions-lgbt_b_9551570

had they listened to their donors. The path forward might not have been easy, but it would have been smoother and less detrimental to the beneficiaries and donor relationships. As Philips described it, all of World Vision's constituents were left in a very confused, disheartened place. Those who disagreed with supporting the LGBT community lost trust in the organization. Donors who felt excited about the change saw how quickly the organization they loved and supported folded under pressure. Everyone lost — most of all, the children in need of sponsorship. The entire thing was an example of disaster via disconnect.

When Stearns reflected on the passionate reaction, he said, "We were trying to find a space of unity beyond the controversies of this issue, and we were unsuccessful in doing it. And we got out ahead of our constituencies, and it really distracted us from our core mission."[24]

Failure to listen to your donors doesn't always lead to a major, public fallout. But it can lead away from your core mission as it did with World Vision. It can happen in smaller ways, too, and when those moments add up, they can have a potentially devastating impact on your relationship with your supporters. Bad spending, focusing on the wrong initiatives, and employee burnout are all symptoms of ignoring your donors, too. While I hope none of this happens to your organization, I guarantee that any organization that fails to listen to its donors will have to face challenges like these.

---

24 Sarah Pulliam Bailey, "World Vision's Rich Stearns: 'A bad decision, but we did it with the right motivations'" Religion News Service, March 27, 2014. https://religionnews.com/2014/03/27/qa-world-vision-president-rich-stearns-sponsors-staff-lost-sex-marriage-announcements/

LISTENING ENCOURAGES LOYALTY

Nonprofits who actively listen to their donors not only avoid alienation, they encourage loyalty. Modern donors want to feel known, understood, and that they are being heard by the people in your organization. *Nonprofit Quarterly* says, "Despite the weight of evidence that it is the single biggest driver of loyalty, few nonprofits actually measure and track levels of donor satisfaction over time."[25] We all seek community and belonging. But it's impossible to build a community without first understanding what is important to people and how to make them happy.

The YMCA is another key example of internal and external complications as a result of not listening to donors. Charles Duhigg outlined their mistake in his book *The Power of Habit*. Duhigg wrote,

> *The accepted wisdom among YMCA executives was the people wanted fancy exercise equipment and sparkling, modern facilities. The YMCA had spent millions of dollars building weight rooms and yoga studios. When the surveys were analyzed, however, it turned out that while a facility's attractiveness and the availability of workout machines might have caused people to join in the first place, what got them to stay was something else. Retention, the data said, was driven by emotional factors, such as whether employees knew members' names or said hello when they walked*

25 Adrian Sargeant, "Donor Retention: What Do We Know & What Can We Do about It?" Nonprofit Quarterly, August 15, 2013. https://nonprofitquarterly.org/donor-retention-nonprofit-donors/

*in. People, it turns out, often go to the gym looking for
a human connection, not a treadmill.*

It's the same theme we see over and over again: People are loyal to
organizations that are proactive about including them. In this case,
people joined the YMCA for the equipment and stayed for the
human connection. Simple acts of personalization were far more
effective in terms of member retention than fancy equipment.

You can't be proactive if you aren't paying close attention. There's
a direct line between understanding your donors and retaining
them. Listening breeds loyalty, because it demonstrates a desire for
the relationship to work on both sides. Simple acknowledgements,
consistency, reliability, and authentic listening are the foundation
of your donor relationships and continued generosity.

FIND THE CONNECTION AND LISTEN INTENTLY

To really understand your donors and execute responsive
fundraising tactics successfully, your nonprofit must dedicate itself
to listening more than you talk. In this hyper-connected world,
your donors are constantly sending signals. Your responsibility is to
keep yourself open to receiving them.

Broadly speaking, we know that email marketing and communications
account for 26 percent of online revenue and that sending donors
to a custom-branded giving page that is nested in your nonprofit's
website will raise six times the amount of money that a non-branded
third-party giving page would yield.[26] Beyond that, web forms and

---

26 Theodore Kinni, "Four Ways Nonprofits Can Increase Their Impact,"
    Insights by Stanford Business, November 1, 2017. https://www.gsb.
    stanford.edu/insights/four-ways-nonprofits-can-increase-their-impact

email engagement provide a wealth of information about your donors' motivations and interests. Using email, web traffic, and web form data is key to listening to modern donors. Your web presence and your ability to easily listen to donor signals in our digital age can be your biggest ally in scaling responsive fundraising strategies.

As you connect with donors, you'll begin to get feedback. This feedback can come directly through one-on-one conversations or indirectly through social listening, website activity, online chat, or email opens and clicks. It comes as a product of choice, too. When you let your donors opt in to the kind of news and content they want to receive from your organization, that's a form of listening. As you listen, you begin to understand areas of interest, their giving opportunities, and how they want to connect and support the cause.

Responsive fundraising is fueled by these signals and equips you to deepen relationships as you move each donor through a journey with your cause. The result is increased donor loyalty, more sacrificial giving and, most importantly, an army of advocates who are intimately connected to your cause.

RESPONSIVE PLAY:
BEHAVIOR-BASED EMAIL SENDS

Email is a powerful, cost-effective way to create a direct connection with your donors. When done right, personalized, automated emails can make the difference between a donor feeling like they are one in a million people, or like they are an integral part of your organization. Here are a few ways to be responsive in your email marketing.

Execute

- Add newsletter subscription call-outs on your website to capture potential donor names. To maximize engagement, use "toast" style animated drop downs or popups when your visitors are leaving the site. These tools are available through Wordpress and other popular platforms. Make sure your call to action focuses on the value that your donor will receive from your emails.

- Write a welcome email series of 3-5 emails that give subscribers and potential donors a brief introduction into the history of your organization, the current programs and initiatives you're running and various ways donors can give to your organization. Onboard new email subscribers with this series rather than throwing them directly into your newsletter flow. This helps educate donors and provide immediate value while they are still thinking about your cause.

- Include a suggested best next action at the end of each email in the series. Save the donate option until the last email to send the message to potential donors that you are dedicated to earning their trust first.

- Monitor conversions on donation pages to ensure those who give before the end of your welcome email series are removed from that sequence before they get asked for a gift and moved into a thank you sequence.

- Automate a thank you sequence of 3 emails, and preferably a phone call, for anyone who converts on your donation pages.

- Write 1-3 different emails to send to donors based on the different milestones they've hit. Include a thank you email for first-time givers, those who hit a monetary or frequency milestone, and those who have returned after a lapse in giving.

- Integrate the thank you email sequence with your automated donor phone call sequence so that you can engage with donors in a multi-channel way.

- Track email engagement at the donor level to gauge which of your donors are opening emails and digging deeper into specific content.

- Make your emails look like they are coming from a person (not your organization) and encourage subscribers to respond with their questions and feedback.

For inspiration in the Listen stage, look no further than giant music streaming service, Spotify. Founded in 2005, Spotify set out to compete with Apple's iTunes. Instead of forcing users to purchase songs, Spotify empowered users to stream high-quality music for free. More importantly, users controlled their own listening experience. While a service like Pandora dictated which songs were played next, and how many times users could skip a song, Spotify allowed users to create their own playlists and jump around to any song they wanted.

The platform found fans quickly, but they did not have the kind of cult following they enjoy now until 2015. That year, the company introduced their famous Discover Weekly playlist. The idea was born from an observation of in-app behavior. What the team noticed was that many users were overwhelmed by the traditional discover page. As music genres started to blend and people were exposed to broader choices, the discover page no longer functioned as an entry to new music. Given too many options, people froze and defaulted back to their old favorites.

The solution was a new personalized, curated playlist populated by algorithms, listening behavior, and information from users around the world. People were hooked instantly. Every Monday, millions of Spotify users opened their personalized Discover Weekly playlist of thirty brand new songs they were sure to love. The enthusiasm caught fire. Not only could Spotify see more people using their app more frequently, but they also noticed a spike in sharing between users.

People loved being able to brag about their exceptional music taste, find new artists before their friends and, most importantly, push play on a trusted playlist before going back to their daily routine. Music reverted back to being a pleasant addition to their commutes and work day rather than a chore they had to monitor every few minutes.

With the success of Discover Weekly, Spotify began releasing all kinds of curated playlists, each one unique to their 217 million users. Spotify offers Daily Mixes and Release Radar for all users. Subscribers receive an added layer of personalization with playlists like The End Of Year which analyzes each person's individual listening habits and presents the information in an immersive event they can experience via email and inside the app.

Unlike the leadership at Kodak in the 1970s, Spotify executives opened themselves up to feedback from all their users. They remained curious, looking for new ways to delight their users with useful features that were relevant to their listening habits. Instead of following the path laid out by iTunes simply because it was the industry leader, they listened to their users directly. They threw out the old playbook and created something that made sense for the people on their platform. They invested time and resources into creating personalized experiences for each of their 75 million individual users. While that time investment was steep in the beginning, they now have the technology to create an immense amount of value to every new user.

Nonprofits need the same hyper-focus on their donors to overcome the generosity deficit they're facing. The tactics used will look different in each organization, but nonprofits that build a comprehensive understanding of their donors' motivations, desires, goals, interests, and loyalties can use that information to bring them closer to the cause.

RESPONSIVE PLAY:
ENGAGE DONORS BASED ON WEB CLICKS

Although online engagements are often the most cost-effective, they are not the only way you should build meaningful relationships with your donors. Leverage the information you gather online to make your in-person conversations most effective. Here's how:

Execute

- Add tracking pixels to your website to see which constituents are engaging with web and email content.

- Use Google Analytics, Virtuous Marketing, or other tools to monitor user behavior including where they came from, pages they visited, time on page, clicks, click-thrus, and where they exited your site. Focus on the projects and pages on your site that are getting the most interest.

- Add website behavior details to your donor profiles to reference during donor calls and personalized email outreach.

- Combine click/open data with comments and likes on your social profiles to see which messaging and topics are getting the most traction.

- Use web clicks to drive donor survey questions, segmentation, messaging or even relevant direct mail pieces in real-time.

- Tie web behavior to marketing automation so that your team knows when to follow up if someone is engaging more deeply in content, or visiting a donation page without giving a gift.

- Make sure to add any relevant context after you've followed up via email or phone call so that your colleagues can use the information to make more targeted engagements in the future.

CHAPTER 7:

IMPROVING YOUR NONPROFIT BY LISTENING TO DONORS

"Successful fundraisers forge ahead and create relationships, trying over time to figure out how a particular donor's interest or foundation's mission might coincide with theirs."

— Jeremy Beer

Crisis Text Line connects people in a moment of crisis with counselors who can offer the resources they need to when they need it. Users send a text to the anonymous number and a volunteer will talk with them until they move from a "hot moment" to a "cool moment." Since 2013, the organization has trained volunteers to support texters through empathetic listening and vetted resources.

Because crises are unpredictable, Crisis Text Line knew they needed volunteers available twenty-four hours a day, seven days a week. In the beginning, that meant setting up volunteers on a weekly schedule. They asked each of their Crisis Counselors to

115

dedicate four hours per week to the platform. Volunteers would sign up for open slots and talk to a handful of people in crisis each shift.

The organization quickly learned that every hour of every day required a different number of volunteers to meet the needs of texters. Often, it was hard to predict, but thanks to the digital nature of the platform, Crisis Text Line started to understand the trends in behaviors and user needs. As you can imagine, talking to someone in the middle of a crisis is a tremendous responsibility. Crisis Text Line couldn't risk overloading volunteers with too many cases. Details could get mixed up, users might feel ignored or, worst of all, someone might make a rash decision in the time they spent waiting for their Crisis Counselor to answer a text.

To support both their volunteers and the texters who relied on them, Crisis Text Line introduced Spike Teams: volunteers who were willing to go above and beyond their four-hour shift could now sign up to be part of an "on-call" group that the platform could connect with during times of significant influx. Holidays, weekend nights, and days of national tragedy tended to trigger more people, and the Spike Team helped keep the queue to a reasonable wait time.

The unintended, but predictable, result of the Spike Team was counselors had an increased commitment to the success of Crisis Text Line. The most engaged volunteers were able to do more when — and if — they wanted to, and they were able to build their own communities within the larger context of volunteers and clients. Soon, each Spike Team had their own name, t-shirts, and inside jokes. Crisis Counselors could recruit new volunteers to their Spike Team, deepening their connection to the community, cause, and organization. Most importantly, the Crisis Text Line was able to make a deeper impact on the texters in need. Soon, they replicated the model in different countries, expanded their reach with new partnerships born of advocacy from the texters and volunteers alike, and have saved millions of lives.

Crisis Text Line listened to their users, analyzed trends, and responded. The change was small at first, an extra team of volunteers to lend a hand during difficult times. But the widespread effects were undeniable. Jeremy Beer explains in his book, *The Forgotten Foundations of Fundraising*, "People give in order to experience belongingness, to shape an identity, and to become more closely connected with others, and not, in the vast majority of cases, to solve social problems or save the world." Crisis Text Line learned this immediately from their Spike Team volunteers, and your nonprofit can too.

The changes that your organization will be able to implement by listening to your donors will be both big and small. You may find new opportunities for extensive new programs, similar to Spotify's platform-wide curated playlists. Or, like Crisis Text Line, you might make a small adjustment that creates a significant ripple effect to your most vulnerable beneficiaries. Both are essential to your sustained growth.

RESPONSIVE PLAY:
CREATE NEXT BEST ACTIONS FROM WEBSITE BEHAVIORS

As you're setting up your infrastructure to allow you to track donor behaviors and listen to signals, it's important to know what you will do with all the new information. Here are a few ways to use the new data.

Execute

- Use conversion rates on the various calls-to-action on your website to understand which donor personas are most likely to convert on your engagements. Even if you have one donation page or form-based landing page you can use query parameters in your email links to attribute donations to specific CTAs. Good email marketing tools and donation software will handle this for you. If not, your favorite neighborhood digital marketer can help set up UTM codes or query parameters so that you can track ROI for each CTA.

- Optimize the donor journey with more relevant CTAs for each persona and lifecycle stage to push donors through the nurture sequences faster. A non-donation CTA (e.g. download our ebook) can be the first small "yes" on the road to a bigger commitment of time or money.

- Leverage a tracking pixel to understand how potential donors move through your website to understand passions, motivations, and information they want most. Create high-value content assets (educational ebooks, issue explainer videos, etc) or automated email series to distribute the information to people and capture new potential donor contact information.

- Create lead-capturing forms to learn a new bit of information from your existing network every time they donate, download, or move through one of your nurture sequences. An additional form to get more information from a donor or give back to a donor can be a useful tool to leverage immediately following a gift.

- Use a dynamic donation page to vary the gift asks and giving arrays based on what you know about donor wealth data, giving capacity, and previous donations. Platforms like Virtuous can help vary the giving array by dynamically looking at the gift history of each donor and changing the ask in real time when someone visits the page.

- Ensure each communication includes trackable URLs to understand the path that donors take when they click away from your communications and onto giving pages, content pages or landing pages.

- Schedule regular reporting meetings with larger teams to ensure that each engagement is converting at the expected pace or better. Implement A/B testing or change the engagement frequency to help make each poor-performing CTA more relevant to donors.

- Update donor personas and donor journey maps with any relevant insights pulled from regular reporting meetings to improve efficiency and generosity.

Definition of Terms

- **Query Parameters and Trackable URLs** - Query parameters is the set information added to the end of a URL that help define the content type or audience in order to understand engagement performance. A trackable URL is the web address link that results from adding query parameters to a URL, which provides information for performance reports.

- **UTM Code** - The set of tags you placed on your tracking links that separates engagement data into clear categories you can use for reporting purposes.

- **A/B Testing** - A strategy in which your nonprofit tests different messages to learn more about what resonates with your donors. Often used in advertisements, websites, and email marketing, teams use engagement metrics to dictate what is more relevant to their audiences. A/B involves sending a percentage of emails or mail pieces to one set of donors and a modified version of the same email/mail to another set of donors to measure which messaging and CTA performs best.

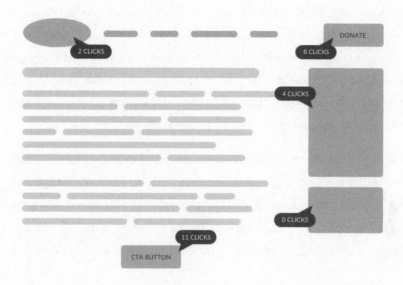

Use behavior data from important landing pages to understand what your donors are most interested in each time they land on your website and what you can provide at the next touchpoint.

REMEMBER: DONORS ARE PEOPLE TOO

I know the power of listening because I've heard success stories and failures from countless donors and nonprofits. And one of my favorite stories came from the most unlikely of places.

My dad is a child of the '60s and, like most of his generation, he's found a home on Facebook. In his younger years, my dad listened to Bob Dylan, hitchhiked across the country, spent time at Haight-Ashbury — the whole nine yards. But, like many in his generation, he's perpetually fifteen years behind on every major technological advancement — except for Facebook.

As part of his Facebook journey, my dad has become one of the most prolific posters that I know. And, like most ex-hippies, his posts are typically equal parts weird and inspiring. For example, a few years ago, my dad invented a fictional horse, and then gave the horse ("Bobby Mac") a separate Facebook profile in order to document its exploits in the golden age of the silver screen cowboys. It was both endearing… and uncomfortably strange.

All that said, as my dad has aged he has become wiser — and increasingly less patient with pretense. Thus, his Facebook posts occasionally include incredibly profound and unfiltered wisdom. A few months ago I came across the post below, and I thought it perfectly summed up two core tenets of responsive nonprofits.

He said,

> Several years ago I was involved with a charity that gave away bicycles at Christmas. On "give away day" we noticed that kids and moms showed up, but not dads. When researched, it was found that dads felt embarrassed and were saddened that they were unable to meet their own child's needs. Their self-respect was shattered. We found a better way to accomplish the goals and still preserve dignity. Here is the point: When the local Television crew or sports hero parades a family in front of the cameras at Christmas time and says, "These people are impoverished and broken, but I saved the day," or "Look at how disadvantaged these folks were until I came along," dignity is tarnished, self-respect diminished. I believe that there is a way to accomplish both the giving and the reception of good works without the embarrassment. Discretion just

takes a little forethought. Please don't think that I am against giving, because that is not the case. Giving is crucial and necessary. Think on humility, graciousness, and self-respect of all concerned when giving a gift. It may allow everyone to fully participate in kindness. Remember, Mr. TV guy or Mr. Sports Star… it's not all about you.

I love this post because, even though it's about the beneficiaries of nonprofit giving rather than the donors, it illustrates three key principles that are crucial for any donor or nonprofit.

1. Listen to Donors, Collaborate and Embrace Change

My dad and his friends, all volunteers, monitored results closely and then made the appropriate changes. They noticed that dads didn't show up and then they researched why. No one brought this concern to them and demanded change. They took it upon themselves to dig deeper. And once the research was analyzed they changed their approach! Remember, my dad was a volunteer and he picked up on something critical the nonprofit missed.

I can't overemphasize the importance of allowing your constituents to help drive innovation and impact. Jeremy Beer noted the same trend in his book *The Forgotten Foundations of Fundraising*: "The fastest-growing, most highly-admired nonprofits invest proportionally more resources into cultivating real relationships with their supporters. They understand that donors are living, breathing people with hopes and dreams and fears, not biped ATMS." The best organizations are the ones that closely measure the results of their program and fundraising efforts and are then willing to listen to the people they serve, the volunteers, and the donors. They then fearlessly change direction to accomplish the mission.

2. It's Not All About You

Whether you're a rich celebrity or a person giving a $10 a month, your gift isn't about you. Yes, you get joy from giving. But you don't get joy because you're a big deal. You get joy from giving because it truly is far better to give than receive. As a charity, it's important that you get to know your donors personally and understand why they give. What motivates them? At the same time, you never want to build an army of donors who believe that their giving is all about them. You want to grow donors who are truly focused on others and swept up in your mission.

3. Everyone Is a Giver

All humans have dignity — and we all have something to give. The biggest financial donors I know often have huge personal needs in other, non-financial areas of their lives. The person you are giving to today might be giving back to you in unexpected ways tomorrow.

Jean Case, the Chief Executive of the Case Foundation, said it best when she said, "I personally refer to Millennials as the next 'Great Generation' because the degree of generosity that we're seeing from them is quite impressive. One common theme among all young people — it was true of Baby Boomers and Gen Xers at this age — they're idealistic.

The big difference, when we began looking at Millennials, is that they're turning their idealism into action in a very real way."[27]

Never use marketing or fundraising tactics that degrade (even unintentionally) the dignity of the givers or receivers at your organization. The negative impact of thoughtless engagements could last for generations.

EMPOWER YOUR DONORS

As you are likely not my dad's friend on Facebook (although you are definitely missing out), a more familiar example of these three principles is the Ice Bucket Challenge made famous in 2014. That summer, millions of people recorded and posted videos where they doused themselves with freezing cold water. Once people recovered from the initial shock of the cold water, they challenged a few of their friends to participate. The choice was simple: post a video of your Ice Bucket Challenge or donate $10 to the ALS Association. Many did both.

The virality of the challenge was remarkable in itself. But many in the nonprofit space marveled at the fact that it wasn't a campaign started by the ALS Association. In fact, when it started, the Ice Bucket Challenge didn't have a specific connection to ALS at all. It wasn't until Chris Kennedy, a professional golfer, told his personal story about a friend who was struggling with ALS that the two

---

27 Brigid Schulte, "Millennials are actually more generous than anybody realizes," *The Washington Post*, June 24, 2015. https://www.washingtonpost.com/news/wonk/wp/2015/06/24/millennials-are-actually-more-generous-than-anybody-realizes/?noredirect=on

were connected.[28] That was in July. By August, the trend was a viral success for the ALS Association.

What the ALS benefited from was the social aspect of human nature, the power of an authentic, personal story, and the democratic way social media puts everyone on the same playing field. It didn't matter if you were Justin Timberlake or my dad. Everyone had a friend who invited them into the global group activity. Each time a video was published, it added to the importance of the movement.

The Ice Bucket Challenge also highlighted how unnecessary nonprofits could be in inspiring generosity. Observant fundraisers saw that sometimes it was better to sit back and let donors create meaning with each other, rather than pushing for their organization to be front and center in the relationship. Your donors need a connection to you in order to give, but they also need a community of people that solidify their internal theories about themselves. They seek proof that other donors are just like them and they can be proud of the tribe of donors they're part of.

A survey by the Pew Research Center found that when Boomers were in their twenties, they held a gloomier view of the future than older generations had. But the reverse is true of Millennials, with this young generation showing the most optimism.[29] In the future, we're going to see more of these global donor-driven initiatives that

---

28 Alexandra Sifferlin, "Here's How the ALS Ice Bucket Challenge Actually Started," *TIME*, August 18, 2014. https://time.com/3136507/als-ice-bucket-challenge-started/

29 "Millennials in Adulthood" Pew Research Center, March 7, 2014. https://www.pewsocialtrends.org/2014/03/07/millennials-in-adulthood/

give them agency and a connection to people in their communities and beyond.

The Ice Bucket Challenge also taught the ALS Association an important lesson in staying agile. The sudden influx of attention and generosity forced them to respond in a meaningful way. They needed to listen to the data, understand the new crop of donors, and figure out strategies to keep them engaged. It was a task they hadn't prepared for, but one that they welcomed.

The more steadfast your organization is in the fundraising strategies of the past, the less likely you'll be able to convert something like the Ice Bucket Challenge into meaningful change. It's also true that a donor-led initiative with the scale of the Ice Bucket Challenge isn't likely to fall into your lap. But if you don't implement the necessary changes to listen to donors, old and new, right now, you will not be set up to leverage the big (and small) donor-driven initiatives of the future. Keep yourself resilient and open to exponential growth by opening communication channels to connect with donors wherever you can.

GET YOUR TEAMS TO START LISTENING

Armed with the knowledge of *why* you need to listen to your donors, the next step is to figure out *how*. The good news is that our connected reality provides ample opportunity to pull data from all of your donors (plus, their friends, family and community members).

Start with what you know about your current donors. Mine your engagement data. Who are your donors today? How are they engaging with your organization and the cause right now? Look beyond RFM (data on the frequency and amount of gifts) into engagements that happen between each gift. Do they love your update emails? Do they only engage with one of your issues and ignore the others? Do they ignore everything until December comes around? Has your cause impacted them in a direct way or did they learn about you from a friend? What information do you repeat too much to them? What are they unfamiliar with? Do they respond better to stories? Or engagement from peers?

Don't settle for putting numbers into a spreadsheet. Create donor profiles based on similar behaviors so you can start to create specific strategies for each donor's journey and experience of your nonprofit. Use the data to ask questions. And then ask even more questions. Don't stop looking for insights about donor behavior. Use the old Toyota principle of "asking *why* 5 times" until you truly understand the core drivers of generosity. Then, get other teams to ask why (and provide their best answers). Remember: The Responsive Framework is a continuous cycle. There are always new donors to get to know, new experiences to provide your existing donors, and new ways to re-engage lapsed donors.

As soon as you have a handle on the information you've already collected, look for new data inputs. Send surveys to your constituents. But do not send the same survey to everyone. It is just as important to personalize the questions as it is to personalize the strategies they inform. If you're struggling to add nuance to the survey questions, collaborate with your major donor representatives. Let them coach you on the different information necessary to move donors to a deeper level of commitment and generosity. They have experience and can help you identify scalable models for each of your individual donors.

Leverage social listening data to understand who your donors are connected with in their community. Listen for how they talk about your nonprofit, who else they support, and what other brands they advocate for. If you can monitor the momentous occasions donors celebrate on their social profiles, you can create additional touchpoints that prove to them that you care about more than just their money. You celebrate them as a complete person, even in the moments that don't have anything to do with your organization.

As your team gets more sophisticated in responsive fundraising strategies, you can start to develop your own listening opportunities. Try creating focus groups based on donor profiles to get direct feedback from different donor segments. Listen for trends that are reflected in your larger donor pool. Ask for their input on new initiatives or campaigns that your team is considering. Listen for praise and criticism at your fundraising and program events. Are there ways to make them more relevant or meaningful to your donors? Who do they serve and how can you expand them to reach more people?

The more comprehensive the data you collect from your donors, the more holistic your responsive fundraising tactics can be. The deeper you can understand what motivates each donor, the more you safeguard yourself against the risks of new ideas. Ultimately, you're hoping to find new ways to inspire generosity and make a bigger impact on the world. That starts by listening to what the people who care most want from you.

CHAPTER 8:

CONNECT: THE ART OF BRIDGING A GAP

"Brag about your donor. Show her results. Tell her she's changing lives and saving people. Give her a reason to know her donation is being used effectively."

– Jeremy Reis

The meteoric rise of Netflix wasn't without consequences. We covered Blockbuster's closing, but the effects of on-demand entertainment spread far beyond America's favorite video rental store. The introduction of streaming services also ignited a culture of "cord cutters:" households that cancelled their subscription to traditional cable channels.

On the surface, the story of Netflix is about how *television* was disrupted. But film — more specifically, the movie-going experience — was fundamentally changed, as well. In 2017, movie attendance in the United States and Canada hit a 25-year low.[30] Although there were an estimated 1.24 billion tickets sold, the number represented a 5.8 percent drop in attendance over 2016.

While streaming services do provide an array of choices that allow users to see more than the blockbuster movies available at their local theater, the real value is in the experience. Movie theaters just don't offer the personalization people need. They dictate which movies we can watch, when, with whom, and even the snacks we are able to enjoy while we watch.

What's worse: movie ticket prices have been on a steady incline since movie theaters first opened their doors.[31] It wasn't that we all agreed that the value of our movie-going experience improved year after year. Rather, we didn't have a lot of power to stop the price hikes from happening. Without any viable alternatives, film enthusiasts forked over more money to see the newest releases.

Netflix saved us by putting us in charge of our own experiences for a consistent monthly price. Not only can we pick from new releases every single week, but we can watch them whenever we want, without worrying about returning them by a certain date or paying extra for late fees. We can stream movies laying in bed or on a rooftop with a big group of friends. Long-distance couples can push play on their laptop to start a movie at the same time while Face-Timing from their phone. Kids can watch quietly in the

---

30   Lizzie Plaugic, "Domestic movie theater attendance hit a 25-year low in 2017," The Verge, January 3, 2018.https://www.theverge.com/2018/1/3/16844662/movie-theater-attendance-2017-low-netflix-streaming

31   "Annual Average U.S. Ticket Price," National Association of Theatre Owners. https://www.natoonline.org/data/ticket-price/

backseat on a long drive using headphones or entire families can share the experience using surround-sound speakers. And, most importantly, we are able to pause or rewind any time we have to use the restroom or make more snacks. The entire thing is personalized in a way that movie theaters cannot compete with.

To their credit, theaters did try. Many movie theaters started switching their old, uncomfortable chairs with electric recliners that give you room to stretch out without fear of kicking the person in front of you. Some allow you to pick your seats ahead of time, to ensure you got the view you wanted. Some even offer cocktails and complete meals delivered directly to your seat. But as we learned from 2017 attendance numbers, the disconnected wasn't with the seats and snacks. It was everything else.

In Phoenix, where my family and I watch movies, our local cinema chain, Harkins Theaters, charges up to $12.50 for a single ticket that isn't an IMAX or 3-D movie. Add that to the $8 popcorn, $5 drinks and $4 candy, things start to add up quickly. That doesn't even include the gourmet food options. All of that might be fine if we could determine when we saw the movie or who else would be at the theater with us. We're paying extra for an experience that is nowhere near what we can create at home. It's just different. It's no longer the exclusive option for watching movies.

The connection between what movie theaters saw (decreased attendance) and how they responded (upgraded seats and snacks) isn't valuable for today's consumer. Ultimately, movie theaters switched from hiking prices to creating a new experience. Too little too late, unfortunately.

Many nonprofits are struggling in much the same way. Many of the organizations that do collect data regularly still don't take the extra step of thinking critically about how the information should inform or evolve their engagement strategies. Organizations continue to send the same messages using the same channels to every donor with little regard for what donors want most.

The danger of unresponsive, disconnected donor relationships isn't simply lower lifetime value. The more perilous risk is actively eroding each donor's relationship with your organization. When you don't respond to their needs, curiosities, and interests in a way that resonates with them, you send a signal that they aren't important to your organization. Of course, you know this couldn't be further from the truth. Donors are the primary reason your organization can exist. But, how would they know that if you're not doing what you can to build that connection?

Giving is deeply personal, and your engagement should be too. Regardless of the channel (website, email, mail, or the phone) or medium (in-person or digitally) you want to connect with donors in a responsive way that feels one-to-one, contextual, and collaborative.

Responsive fundraising ensures you connect with the right donors at the right time with the right message. It allows you to personalize the experience every time you connect with every donor. When they visit your website, attend an event, receive an email or get a phone call, each person should feel like they are part of an ongoing conversation with your organization. This builds connection and increases trust.

Sound impossible? Don't lose heart. This is where new technology (data-driven CRM and automation) and a responsive mindset work together to help you connect personally with all your donors.

THE POWER OF MARKETING AUTOMATION

When I talk to nonprofits about personalizing communication to each donor, their response is typically something like, "We have an incredibly limited staff and even more limited time. There's no way that we create this type of personal connection."

In one sense they are right. It's functionally impossible to have a staff member build a deep relationship with every donor, and then respond in an authentic way.

But in another sense, personalized communication at scale is very much within reach of your nonprofit. Ready for a shocker? The same tools that Amazon and Netflix use to create personalized experiences are available to you.

The staff at Netflix doesn't *actually* know what you want to watch next. They don't have individual team members reaching out to members and asking what shows they like and what they want to see more of. But they are able to leverage predictive data analytics to make a great guess at your new favorite show. They then use a marketing automation platform to send you texts and emails to drive you to the perfect product at the exact right time.

As I've been saying, this technology has been a driving force for the downfall of brands like Sears and the rise of online retailers. The power of Amazon and other online retailers isn't simply that they exist on the internet. The real power of digital commerce is that it enables retailers to create a truly personalized experience.

I remember receiving the Sears catalog in the mail as a kid. The catalog came once a year and included everything from clothes to appliances to toys. As fun as it was to flip through the catalog, it rarely intersected with our family's purchasing needs in real-time. But in 2020, with the help of tools Shopify, Drift, and Marketo, my favorite online retailers send me exactly the right product recommendation at exactly the right time. Because these suggestions are so incredibly relevant, I'm willing to give retailers permission to market to me as frequently as they wish. Rather than the one-to-many experience of a Sears catalog, I'm getting hyper-personalized messages through marketing automation that drive increased response.

Keep in mind: catalogues aren't dead; they're just a different experience. Like movie theaters, they're adapting in order to survive.

At its heart, marketing automation allows you to build a sequence of marketing activities that are automatically triggered when a particular action happens in your database. You can think of it as an AI assistant that does all the personalized follow up that you'll never have time for, but donors want. Stanford Graduate School of Business professor Walter W. Powell encourages early adoption of practices devoted to strategic planning, operational efficiencies, and progress measurement. He said, "This is what, in part, has helped [nonprofits] reach out to their constituents through the web and share data on the impact of their work."

He mentioned that younger donors, especially, are interested in "high-impact philanthropy" and want nonprofits to use for-profit metrics to measure impact.[32] This type of hyper-personalized impact reporting and storytelling can only happen at scale through they power of marketing automation.

For example, let's say that you want to make sure that donors who give to your "Scholarship for a Child" project get a special thank you. You can design a workflow that automatically sends three emails, one email staggered every three days, each providing project-specific content and videos to each donor. Marketing automation simply makes note of new gifts and starts the sequence when each donation comes in. In effect, you're providing personalized experiences for each donor in real time, much like the experience you would get from Amazon.

I recently spoke with Tracy Bumpus from Intend Ministries. I asked her about the creative campaigns her organization was executing using technology to serve their supporters. Tracy proceeded to tell me an incredibly compelling story of how her nonprofit was able to give back to donors.

In advance of the hurricanes in the Carolinas, Intend Ministries took the initiative to give to their donors rather than just asking/getting. Intend isn't in fthe "relief and development" space (they are a faith-based media nonprofit) but they still wanted to serve their constituents affected by the storms the best way they could.

---

32   Louise Lee, "When Nonprofits Act Like Businesses, Transparency Improves," Insights by Stanford Business, May 5, 2017. https://www.gsb.stanford.edu/insights/when-nonprofits-act-businesses-transparency-improves

Rather than tell you the story in my words, I've included Tracy's story below in her own words. Notice how Tracy is leveraging technology to personalize donor communication and give first before getting back. Hopefully this story inspires creativity and helps all of us seek ways to better serve those around us.

> We used our CRM's map function in each contact record to help us identify donors and other individuals in Florida and North Carolina who have been in the paths of incoming hurricanes in both 2017 and 2018. With our location in middle Tennessee, we are accustomed to being an evacuation point for the southern Atlantic coast and the Gulf Coast. Five individual interstates intersect here so we are a destination for evacuees.
>
> We were concerned about our donors and contacts who were in the paths of these storms, especially those who are elderly and isolated. Being proactive and serving our broadcast audience is important to us, so we ran a query to find donors in those states and neighboring states that might be impacted by the storms.
>
> Rather than trying to narrow down coastal locations by zip codes which would have involved more significant research, we simply looked at the map of locations of contacts in our CRM to determine exactly where the contacts were located in terms of geography. If a contact was near the coast or an inland river where storm surge might be an issue, we moved them to a queue. We picked up the phone and reached out

in order to make sure they had a plan in place and to pray with them. For all others, we sent an email letting them know we were praying for them and to let them know we stood ready to welcome them in our location. We also offered to reserve hotels rooms on their behalf at the local properties where we have corporate rates if they decided to head for the higher ground of Middle Tennessee.

Good data analytics and marketing automation systems also allow you to listen for activity on your website and other marketing initiatives then connects them with the data you already have. Organizations like Intend are able to identify donor behavior or attributes that demand specific action, and then use automation to schedule calls, send physical mail, or generate a series of emails with limited effort from their staff. These systems help make sense of the activities of large numbers of individuals by bubbling them up to you. Next steps for each donor can be driven by their engagement with web content, their attendance at events or their volunteer activity. It also allows you to automatically communicate based on those specific moments, allowing you to be responsive without having staff spend all day monitoring and responding to what's happening.

RESPONSIVE PLAY:
AUTOMATION FOR NURTURING A FIRST TIME DONOR

Fundraisers of all experience levels know that re-engaging existing donors is easier (and less expensive) than finding new donors. To help keep existing donors engaged with your nonprofit, and primed to give again, here are a few ways to automate and streamline your efforts.

Execute

- Create automated tasks to make a one-on-one connection with donors within 14 days of their first gift.

- Turn on a welcome/thank you email series of 3-4 emails.

- Subscribe donors to monthly engagement emails based on indicated interests, passions, programs that matter to them.

- Automate a "Welcome Package" physical letter designed to educate givers and tell stories of impact to arrive within 14 days of first gift.

- If there gift is under $300 and the donor engages with your digital content, send an email after 28 days to encourage the donor to participate in your monthly giving program tied to specific impact.

- If donor has high engagement and is an influencer (i.e. has over 100 Twitter followers, has high density of donors in their neighborhood) follow up with a personal email to let them know how to become an advocate for your cause.

- Track engagement behaviors, automatically enrolling donors in a pre-lapse engagement campaign when they have ignored your connection efforts for six months. Provide valuable content, impact stories, and new opportunities to get involved.

- Enroll donors in a re-engagement workflow, including online and offline engagements, if they do not respond to the pre-lapsed automation workflow. Keep an eye on engagement behaviors and conversion metrics.

- Automate a personalized phone call from your team when a donor re-engages and gives another time.

- Pull reports on pre-lapse engagement campaign and re-engagement campaign to understand which donor personas respond to what messaging. Test new information against what you know from social, direct mail, and other offline engagements to come up with new content that is relevant to donors.

Automation workflows make it simple to understand the next best action for each individual donor. The result is an efficient team connecting with all donors in a meaningful way.

RESPONSIVE PLAY:
ADD GEO-LOCATION AND SOCIAL INFLUENCE TAGS TO DONOR PROFILES

Access to a donor's address is one thing. But understanding where that donor lives, what that region of the country might mean for their giving motivations, and who else in your network might be close by is the valuable information you can use to inspire generosity and loyalty. Here are a few tags that can be added to your donor profiles to give your team more context.

Execute

- Use geo-location to determine the density of donors in a particular area. Allow major donor reps and event coordinators to plan based on where your donors naturally live.

- Use event attendance data combined with geo-location/address to determine where your organization has the most traction. Use this data to inform your donor acquisition efforts, future events and peer-to-peer campaigns.

- Use social influence data to identify your top advocates for the cause. Influence data should include social media following, peer-to-peer fundraising engagement, employment/church information, and number of relationships with other donors. This data can be used to highly target communications for advocacy efforts like posting on behalf of the cause, raising awareness for an event, or hosting a peer-to-peer campaign.

- Use marketing automation to listen for these insights in your database and automatically add donor tags, notify your team, or send email/mail to engage in a relevant way.

More than Just Email and Web: A Comprehensive Approach

Technology tools are important, but they're only one part of responsive fundraising. Driving personal connections goes far deeper than emails, text messages and website visits. In-person events, handwritten notecards, one-on-one meetings and phone calls still have a huge role to play in inspiring generosity. In fact, these traditional tactics can often have a much larger impact than their digital counterparts. We find that the most effective nonprofits use multi-channel automation to drive personalized communication streams across:

- Direct Mail
- Email
- Text
- One-on-One Meetings
- Calls
- Events
- Receipts

Rather than thinking in terms of annual campaigns that run once and end, responsive nonprofits monitor engagement and acknowledge that each person is at a different point in their donor journey.

For example, let's say two donors gave the exact same amount, $100, to your recent campaign. The first donor has given many times before to similar initiatives, but the second donor has only donated once before. You could send them both the same thank you for their donation, and stop there. But that won't appeal to the long-term loyalty of modern donors. Knowing more about them and their engagement with your organization thus far, you are able to get more personal. Maybe you follow up with the second donor with a phone call to thank them personally and welcome them to your organization. Meanwhile, your first donor might be funneled into a series of emails telling them about upcoming campaigns they might be interested in based on previous programs they've donated to.

Automated communication combined with good listening allows donors to progress at the right pace. The result is more loyal, engaged donors who feel a personal connection to the cause.

Responsive Direct Mail

One of the most misunderstood connection fundraising tactics is direct mail. Yes, direct mail can be misused (i.e. sending the exact same institutional appeal to every single person in your database), but direct mail is not a fundamentally bad tactic. In fact, it remains one of the most important fundraising tactics available to nonprofits. It's all in how you use it.

I can't tell you the number of times I've sat in a nonprofit board meeting or planning meeting and heard an unsophisticated board member say, "Why are we still sending mail? It's a waste of money, nobody wants mail!" Before they are even finished with their sentence, the head of direct response will fire back, "We use it because it works! 70 percent of our giving comes through direct mail!" The argument then devolves into a debate about whether mail is fundamentally good or evil, without much nuance or context.

In our new, complex reality, arguing about the value of direct mail doesn't serve anyone well. Like any tactic, direct mail *can* deliver valuable results if it's leveraged in a way that draws donors closer to your cause and inspires loyalty.

Email is one of the most cost-effective ways to cut through the noise of other communication channels and connect directly to your donors. But, the relatively inexpensive nature of email also means many nonprofits forgo quality for quantity. As a result, our email inboxes are a cluttered mess of marketing emails and impersonal prospecting attempts. On the other hand, our physical mailboxes are much less crowded and easier to break through, especially when you've mailed a piece driven by marketing automation and data insights. You're able to ensure direct mail is both relevant and value-based according to the behaviors of each donor.

A particularly powerful version of direct mail is letters-on-demand through marketing automation. Rather than blasting everyone on your file with the same piece of mail, letters-on-demand allows you to automatically send the right letter at the right time with no additional work from your staff. So, for example, rather than dumping a new donor into your typical mail stream, they might get a three-piece welcome series arriving seven, thirty, and sixty days after their first gift. The series could introduce them to the cause over time, rather than expecting them to jump into an existing conversation right away.

When I suggest this approach to nonprofits, I often hear, "There's no way we could approach mail this way! This would exponentially increase the demand on our employees' time and double our cost per mail piece." But with marketing automation this approach is far less time consuming than you think and has the potential to generate incredibly high ROI.

Let me share the true value of the return on strategic, responsive connection costs.

TYPICAL DIRECT RESPONSE APPEAL

Recipients: Everyone who has given in the last 18 months. Total of 10,000 individuals.

ROI Calculation:

Internal Cost to Produce and Approve Monthly Appeal	$5,000
Cost of Direct Mail Pieces ($1 x 10,000 donors)	$10,000
Total Cost	**$15,000**
Response Rate	7%
Average Gift	$50
Total Revenue	$35,000
Net Revenue After Costs	$20,000
Final ROI	**75%**

RESPONSIVE DIRECT RESPONSE APPEAL

Recipients: Targeted donors identified by engagement behaviors and donor journey stage via direct mail marketing automation workflow. Total of 7,000 individuals.

ROI Calculation:

Internal Cost to Produce and Approve Monthly Appeal	$10,000
Cost of Direct Mail Pieces ($2 x 7,000 donors)	$14,000
Total Cost	**$24,000**
Response Rate	18%
Average Gift	$70
Total Revenue	$88,200
Net Revenue After Costs	$34,800
Final ROI	**153%**

In the second scenario, you send less mail but the mail that you do send is hyper-relevant based on each donor's behavior and stage in the donor journey. Even though you're sending less volume, you can still drive a greater response rate and a greater average gift amount because you are asking for the right thing at the right time. The targeted approach to direct mail can have a profound impact on the ROI of the campaign and revenue directed to the cause.

COMBINE LISTENING WITH A PERSONAL CONNECTION

To see The Responsive Framework in action, consider the success of Dollar Shave Club. From the beginning, founder Michael Dubin was a living example of the responsiveness. The idea started in 2011 when a family friend mentioned a warehouse full of razors he needed to unload. Dubin knew that American men were evolving and he could turn the surplus razors into a community.

He said, "Five years ago, if you spent time in front of the mirror, people would have called you a metrosexual. We now live in the age where it's OK to hug guys and compliment and give advice."[33] So, he created a system where men could receive the tools they needed to take care of their appearance the way they wanted to. But it was what happened next that really illuminates the importance of direct connection to individuals who support your organization.

After the launch, Dubin realized that while men had access to razors and other grooming products, what they needed, and weren't

---

33 Jaclyn Trop, "How Dollar Shave Club's Founder Built a $1 Billion Company That Changed the Industry" Entrepreneur, March 28, 2017. https://www.entrepreneur.com/article/290539

getting, was a place to get real-time answers to their grooming questions. He saw a way to capitalize on the "club" portion of Dollar Shave Club.

Dubin created a role for himself as the company's first Club Pro. His take on customer service, a Club Pro would be on hand to answer both questions about orders and grooming and personal care. It functioned as a personalized concierge experience, available on all channels — email, phone, text, chat or social media. No matter what the question was, Dubin would find the answer and offer advice to men when they needed it. Once hooked, Dollar Shave Club could send automatic targeted emails based on their knowledge of each respondent's stage in the buyer journey.

As *Entrepreneur* tells it, "Once Dubin hired a few employees, he and a small team began traveling the country to learn more about people's grooming habits. They focused on regional events like the Maine Lobster Festival and the Gilroy Garlic Festival — places where grooming conversations weren't exactly the norm. The point was to meet average guys on their turf and learn what they wanted. 'We figured out how to talk to people, not at them,' said Cassie Jasso, one of the company's first 10 hires."

That early adoption of active customer engagement, online and off, and meaningful responses led to Dubin selling Dollar Shave Club for $1 billion dollars in 2016 — just five years later.

This kind of holistic engagement is a philosophy that you must model in your organization. Nonprofits have perfected the art of comprehensive engagement for major donors, but it breaks down with everyday donors. Direct mail efforts and Facebook ads from a single nonprofit often fall into two categories. They either are exactly the same message or they look like they could be from two separate organizations.

The Cornell Lab of Ornithology adopted a responsive fundraising strategy as they sought ways to engage new audiences. Instead of relying on rented attention (i.e. paying for ad space, thus renting that audience for a short time) and mass-blast attacks (i.e. sending volumes of impersonal communication and hoping that someone responds), they looked at the challenge from a different angle.

They mined their audience and donor signals to identify areas of interest and need that overlapped with the lab's expertise. The goal wasn't to find donor needs and then create new capabilities. That would take too much time and effort and had the potential to steer them away from their core goals. Instead, they focused on the intersection between donor interests and their existing strengths to make a valuable connection.

What they found was a growing interest in bird facts — specifically bird sounds. Luckily, the lab had stacks of information about different bird sounds. So, they created a series of landing pages with downloadable bird sounds and the Merlin Bird ID app, which people could download for free. The app, accompanied with a target ad campaign, multi-channel communications plan, and marketing automation, allowed The Cornell Lab to connect with tens of thousands of new people and ultimately engage them to become donors. During one campaign in 2015, they connected with nearly 120,000 people, had 52,086 downloads of

Merlin Bird ID, and generated $62,000 in gifts through hyper-personalized, targeted nurture sequences.[34]

Similar to Dollar Shave Club, Cornell sought to understand the challenges of their target audience and then identify ways they could show up and serve these needs. This use of content marketing leverages the responsive framework in a way that earns attention, builds trust, and grows loyalty.

DON'T FORGET TO GET PERMISSION

Responsive fundraisers seek to build lasting relationships, and healthy relationships are two-way streets. *They require permission.* In the digital era of nonprofit apps, websites, emails, and texts, a person must always opt-in to learn more about your organization. Permission means your communication and engagement will be anticipated and relevant.

Permission within marketing and communications was popularized in Seth Godin's book, *Permission Marketing*, where he called out brands and direct marketers for overlooking customer desires with mass-blast tactics that sought to steal attention, rather than earn it. He pointed to a future when customers wouldn't tolerate this any longer, because they had the power of choice. That was 1999. I'd argue that Godin's future is right now.

---

34 Case Study: Cornell Lab of Ornithology, Media Cause. 2019. https://mediacause.org/our-work/case-study/online-fundraising-program-generates-4-million/

The General Data Protection Regulation, passed by the European Union in 2016, was the first law that required international companies to take permission seriously for their customers. It gave individuals control over what they share, with what companies and when. Businesses were forced to adjust their data collection tactics immediately. More importantly, they will have to prioritize permission and transparency for the foreseeable future. Despite new laws, ignorance and disbelief around permission among marketers is still too common.

What constitutes permission? Well, the fact that the answer is debatable is half the problem. Marketers are often lost looking for the line and wondering how far they can push without crossing it. As a general rule, if you don't know for sure that you have permission to engage, assume you don't. To get a broad understanding, start with the five types of permission that Godin curated for us twenty-plus years ago:

- Situational permission
- Brand trust
- Personal relationship
- Customer permission
- Intravenous permission

I won't dig into the particulars of each of these permission types in this book, but I highly encourage you to search out Godin's work if you're unsure about how your organization is asking for permission and gaining trust.

If you seek an open, mutually beneficial relationship with donors, you should go deeper. In his book *The New Nonprofit*, Nicholas Ellinger calls nonprofits to go further with permission and seek channel permission or communication preferences.

He argues that a donor who gave permission to email did not also agree to mail, texts, or calls. Ellinger believes that to ignore channel or communication permissions inevitably leads to lower returns.

"Just as beauty is in the eye of the beholder, spam is in the eye of the recipient: if it is a message I didn't want, it is spam. Non-desired messages hurt your ability to reach your audience. ...By asking for preferences and honoring them, you not only identify those quality donors — you make them more likely to stay by listening and acting to serve them."

I couldn't agree more. Permission is a process of listening, not a single moment. As you listen to donor signals, you must continually ask, "have we been given permission to respond? In what way would our response be appropriate?" It sounds like a big undertaking, but just like in any relationship, this kind of thinking can quickly become habitual the more you practice it over time.

CHAPTER 9:

BUILDING AUTHENTICITY AND TRUST THROUGH CONNECTION

"If you need to raise funds from donors, you need to study them, respect them, and build everything you do around them."

– Jeff Brooks

If you missed the Fyre Festival, congratulations. You successfully avoided a major scam. The 2017 festival was promoted as a pairing of Instagram's most important influencers with the best music acts on a private island in the Bahamas. After a few posts from the most popular celebrities went online, organizers watched as the crowds (and the dollars) came pouring in. Groups of young people forked over thousands to be part of an exclusive weekend of luxury and entertainment.

Except, it never happened. The festival didn't deliver on any of the promises it made to ticket holders. Hundreds of people lost their money and were left stranded on an island with little food, shelter, or way out. You can watch the whole thing unfold in *Fyre: The Greatest Party That Never Happened* on Netflix or *Fyre Fraud* on Hulu. As interesting as both documentaries are, the heart of the story, and why I bring it up here, lies with Maryann Rolle.

Rolle is a local Bahamian restaurant owner who was commissioned to feed all Fyre Festival attendees. When the festival didn't happen, all of her work — the time she spent organizing and planning, the food she ordered, everything — was for nothing. When the dust settled, Rolle, a kind, hard-working woman, was left with a $100,000 debt the Fyre Festival executives were not going to pay. Watching her tell her story in the documentary is both heartbreaking and infuriating.

Days after Netflix released the documentary, a woman named Pamela Carter opened a GoFundMe campaign for viewers to help Rolle. Within a few days, the campaign was completely funded, eventually raising over $230,000 from over 9,000 individuals.[35]

Carter knew that many people shared an intense desire to do something about the awful way Rolle was treated and immediately created an opportunity. She opened a direct connection between people who felt passionate about the injustice and a specific beneficiary. Carter listened and then told a relevant, timely story in an authentic way and the results were undeniable.

---

35   https://www.gofundme.com/f/exuma-point-fyre-fest-debt

The strategy didn't take a year of planning and approvals. Carter simply listened to the conversation happening on social media, created an opportunity to make a positive impact, and made the connection on the same channels. Where unresponsive fundraisers might observe a trend but ignore it in favor of more "tried and true" strategies, responsive fundraisers know that now is the time to act to create the most good in the world.

FOCUS ON RELEVANT, TIMELY CONTENT

Derrick Feldman, president and founder of Achieve, found similar trends as Carter. He said, "We're finding you still have to activate [Millennials] to get on board to do something. Yes, technology is an exciting tool. But to move someone to action still requires a messenger, a message, and a purpose."

Ellinger echoed his sentiment in *The New Nonprofit*. He wrote, "It's a bit heretical, but less volume can sometimes mean more revenue. Looking at a US charity that mails about twice a month, 75% of additional mail pieces' revenues weren't new revenues. Thus any mail piece with standalone ROI less than 300% is a net loser for them."

Unless you know your communication is relevant, action-oriented, and meaningful to your donors, there is no reason to send it.

One benefit to this more time-sensitive, relevant approach is the ability to talk more frequently with your donors. I've had organizations tell me that "our donors don't want more than four emails per year." Often what they mean is "our donors only want four impersonal, irrelevant institutional fundraising emails per year." Often those same donors are getting six to ten emails a week from Amazon, LinkedIn, or their favorite clothing companies. Yet they rarely complain or unsubscribe. These emails never seem like a burden because they consistently provide real, timely value to their recipients. The more you can provide hyper-relevant value, the more you'll have permission to speak into the lives of donors.

RESPONSIVE PLAY:
SOCIAL INFLUENCERS, PEER-TO-PEER FUNDRAISING AND ADVERTISING SUPPORT

Social media is an incredibly powerful tool that many nonprofits fail to leverage in the right ways. Whether you want to use influencers to spread your message, recruit peer-to-peer fundraising candidates, or simply reach new people, here are a few ways your organization can be more responsive on social media.

Execute

- A/B test messaging on Facebook to ensure optimization and messaging that resonates. A/B testing stories, content, and CTAs on Facebook can be the easiest, most inexpensive way to optimize your message before an event, web update or large mail piece. Start by creating two visually similar ads with a different headline you'd like to test. A/B test the ads with the same audience (half see one ad, half see the other). Watch which ad gets the most traction. Update the ads, iterate and try again.

- Ask an interesting question of your audience in at least half of your posts on social. Questions on social and online communities like Quora help solicit real feedback from your audience and give your fans a voice within their communities.

- Use social media data in your CRM to understand which influencers are most relevant and important to each of your donor personas. Scrape social profiles to see each donor's social footprint, track followership, and integrate their Twitter feed into each donor's profile.

- Activate a partnership with important social influencers to advocate for your cause. Send audiences to a custom-branded landing page or send them direct mail pieces to learn about your organization and take the next steps in advocating for your cause.

- Designate a point person on your staff to equip influencers and assign them a task to reach out when a new influencer is auto-tagged in your database.

- When possible, segment influencers by type (e.g. Pastor, Social Media Maven, Policy Influencer, etc) and provide unique calls to action for each.

- Identify highly-connected donors in your database to enroll into a P2P fundraising recruiting workflow. Suggest each person advocate and share P2P initiatives for your nonprofit to their networks online and offline. When possible, provide influencers with pre-packaged social posts, notecards, etc to share in order to take the friction out of their communication.

- Deploy social media advertisements and promoted posts to potential donors and current donors to offer high-value content they can download, share, and use to recruit their friends.

- Match the donor journey for each persona with highly-relevant social ads that will help convert them into first- or second-time donors. You can use donor email addresses to target specific donors on Facebook or Instagram based on a particular stage in the donor journey.

- Use lookalike audiences in social advertising to drive new audiences to your social influencer campaigns and the associated landing pages that convert new audience members into potential donors ready to learn more.

- Use geo-targeting tags to create a smaller groups of donors to advocate for your cause in their communities. Link them with social influencers to grow the impact of each event.

- Pull engagement data to understand which influencers you can create lasting partnerships with and what new influencers you should start working to connect with.

Definition of Terms

- **Lookalike Audiences** - A group of individuals that Facebook identifies based on demographic data pulled from a segmented list of donors. Facebook allows you to upload a set of current contacts and then finds other people who "look like" those contacts. The individuals in this group behave like your current donors, care about similar causes, and have been identified by Facebook as candidates who will most likely take the desired action you're hoping for.

- **Social Ad Targeting** - The act of advertising to donors, potential donors, and new individuals through social channels in order to bring awareness to your nonprofit or drive conversions on your landing pages. Ad retargeting allows you to track the behavior of your donors on the internet and then serve them ads on Facebook, Google, etc. specific to their previous web activity. This is the engine that drives many of the "magically" personalized ads you see when browsing online.

- **Geo-Targeting** - The act of sending specific messaging, content, or advertisements to a specific group based on where they live or the locations they tend to frequent. It can even include a one-time target around an event, like the Boston Marathon, for example.

THE POWER OF AUTHENTIC STORYTELLING

The proliferation of the internet search, smartphones, and user-contributed content means that modern donors have exponentially more access to information now than they did at any other time in human history. And, because social platforms amplify everyone's voice, you can no longer contain your message to only your website or direct mail list. The democratization of information empowers modern donors to stay informed and act quickly. They often come to your organization with an opinion on your cause that has been formed by friends, curated news feeds, and whatever random pundit that may have an opinion of your mission.

William Schambra summarized the stunning findings of Money for Good when he said only 35 percent of donors ever do any research, and almost three-quarters of those who do spend less than two hours at it. Additionally, of those who do research, 63 percent use it only to confirm that the organization they've chosen isn't a total fraud.[36]

This doesn't mean that donors are giving haphazardly and without reason. It means that their peers, families, faith communities, etc have largely influenced their decision long before they show up on your website or see your direct mail piece.

In order to thrive in this new world, it's imperative that your organization creates authentic stories that resonate with donors, and then distributes those stories where your fans and advocates are already spending time. It's no longer sufficient to publish institutional content on your website and hope that donors find you. Responsive nonprofits create content that informs and empowers donors within the forums in which they are already talking.

---

36 Money for Good 2015: Revealing the voice of the donor in philanthropic giving. Camber Collective. http://www.cambercollective.com/moneyforgood

I mentioned Scott Harrison earlier, and no nonprofit does this better than charity:water. In some ways, many nonprofits are sick of hearing about charity:water. They've become the defacto example that staff and agencies refer to when they talk about good fundraising. That said, the praise is justified and can't be ignored. Their superb storytelling builds unparalleled connections with donors that has garnered tremendous success over the last decade. On their website, they dedicate an entire section to success stories of beneficiaries and donors' generosity. Visitors can scroll through each beautifully documented story, or refine their experience to the countries they're most interested in. Most stories are told through text and videos, giving donors a variety of ways to build a connection.

But they don't stop at their website. Scott regularly speaks at nonprofit conferences, on podcasts and at private events. He's even written a book explaining the work that is made possible by donors around the world.

In addition, charity:water works particularly hard to offer social proof for donors and potential donors throughout their social media. They use a variety of opportunities to encourage their donors to share the story of charity:water. Whether they leverage the moment right after giving or immediately following a video view, the team at charity:water ensures that there is always a new way for their organization to connect to potential new donors and expose a wider audience to the ways in which these individuals can impact water crisis.

What charity:water proves is that modern nonprofits need a clear strategy to tell authentic stories that your donors want and believe in. Responsive nonprofits know the impact is in the connection to their donors, not the money spent or frequency of engagements.

BUILDING TRUST AND CONNECTION

The reason people can trust a brand like charity:water over others boils down to active participation in connection. Unresponsive nonprofits fall into a pattern that is comfortable and familiar to them. They lean away from active participation in everyday donor relationships because, on some level, they think they have inherent relevance or value to donors that doesn't require a personal connection. The responsive team at charity:water, however, knows that that will never be true. Donors will always want more transparency. Every time they give, they want a closed loop for their generosity. Not only because they want confirmation that you are the right organization to trust with their generosity, but also because they care deeply that something positive is happening with their favorite cause.

RESPONSIVE PLAY:
CLOSE THE LOOP WITH DONORS THROUGH AUTOMATION

Silos within your nonprofit prevent your donors from moving closer to the impact they are helping create. Until you can successfully integrate the work your team does across departments, an easy fix to be more responsive to your donors is to automate communication that closes the loop for donors. Here's a quick workflow you can add to your process right now.

Execute

- Identify milestones in your current projects and programs that donors have indicated interest in.

- Create tasks that your team can execute once those milestones have been hit (calls, personal emails, cards, etc).

- Allow staff working in the field or program to provide updates on projects directly in your donor software.

- Segment audience members based on their interest in each milestone and preferred communication style.

- Automatically send out communications and schedule project content to go live once your field team has indicated that the milestones have been met.

- Publish social media posts to celebrate project milestones.

- Write contingency emails, social media posts, and direct mail pieces for when your team gets stuck on a particular milestone or does not reach a goal in the allotted time. Include suggestions for helping push your team over the line or explain how you will modify your strategy to reach each milestone in the future. Don't be afraid to admit failure! Authenticity and trust are built through this type of communication.

- Pull behavior reports after each send to understand what content was most read, most relevant, and most important for each donor persona.

> • Optimize the next milestone communication to better close the loop by providing better, more relevant information.

Donors appreciate the effort nonprofits go to in order to maintain a deep, meaningful connection that reflects their own passion for the cause. Kathleen, a donor we spoke to while researching this book, echoed the common sentiment perfectly when she talked about her connection to The Sea Turtle Preservation Society. As a Florida resident, the issue of unprotected sea turtles is something she can see every day from her own backyard. As a frequent visitor of a nearby reserve, Kathleen wanted to do more to help protect the sea turtles that brought her and her family so much joy.

She gave money and time, volunteering to mark off nests to protect turtles from human interference. But it wasn't until Kathleen saw The Sea Turtle Preservation Society make a comprehensive strategy that she found where she could do the most good in her community. She said, "Not only do they act on the causes we care about (beach clean-ups, education around reusable products, rehabilitation for turtles and policy advocacy), but they show us every time they put our donations back into our local agencies, which preserve the safe havens for three species of sea turtles."

Kathleen picked up on the relevant connections that the responsive fundraisers at The Sea Turtle Preservation Society had implemented. Their approach, much like charity:water, was multifaceted because they understood the different needs of their donors. They ensured that donors had a way to connect deeply with the work of the organization regardless of whether or not they cared about policy change or rehabilitation or any of it.

Daniel Ames put it best when he said, "When people feel 'listened to' by would-be agents of influence their liking for, commitment to, and trust in the agents tend to increase, thereby expanding the agents' influence."[37]

In order to cultivate this kind of loyalty and influence, your organization must first understand all the ways your donors want to be connected to you. Listen for cues about which channels are most relevant, which programs inspire the most passionate engagements, and what your nonprofit work looks like to donors in the future. Then connect with each donor in a personal way as you work together to find the most meaningful connection points.

Think about where you will connect with each of your donor segments and what you will say to prove that you are listening and responding to their needs. Enlist the help of different teams to pull stories of successes and obstacles you haven't been able to overcome on your own. Take an inventory of everything you can provide to your donors in order to fill in the gaps where you see them.

Remember, The Responsive Framework isn't a fixed set of action items. It's an ever-evolving process that you are constantly cycling through. What builds a connection with new donors now might not work in five years. What is your plan to foster internal

---

37   Money for Good 2015: Revealing the voice of the donor in philanthropic giving. Camber Collective. http://www.cambercollective.com/moneyforgood

collaboration so you're always optimizing your operations, fundraising and marketing to improve donor relationships? If you can implement a process now, you will protect yourself from falling dangerously behind the trends in the future.

CHAPTER 10:

USING SUGGESTIONS TO GROW RELATIONSHIPS

"There are two i's in fundraising. They should stand for inspiration and innovation, not imitation and irritation."

– Ken Burnett

My wife loves the winter. More specifically, she loves winter fashion. This year, she decided that she wanted to find the perfect pair of snow boots to accentuate her impeccable fashion sense during our winter vacation plans. She knew she wanted a pair of Sorel boots, but wasn't quite sure which pair.

Rather than use our home computer, she opened my laptop to browse through her options, hoping to find the perfect boots. Ultimately, she ended up buying a pair at the mall and didn't make an online purchase. The problem is, Sorel didn't follow her purchasing behavior, nor were they able to recognize that my wife had used my computer. So, for the next two weeks, no matter where I went online, there was a picture of the boots my wife had viewed.

Retargeting ads can be a powerful tool to push consumers when they are undecided on a product. But, it only works if the company using the retargeting ads has a strategy in place rooted in relevance. The fact that my wife was using my computer didn't register for Sorel, much less that we already made our offline purchase. They just knew my computer browsed their site. They listened for one signal (website visits), but didn't do the work to connect that information with my profile. Thus, their suggestion was "Buy NOW" on boots I couldn't wear.

This kind of badgering without context isn't confined to display ads. It bleeds into email inboxes too. The most grating example that comes to mind is Casper Mattress. Scott, a long-time member of the Virtuous team, bought a mattress from Casper earlier this year. He was intrigued by their obvious focus on customer service and experience. Not only could he skip the in-store buying process in favor of a simple online shopping experience, he also knew he was getting a quality product that would be delivered quickly. What started out as a customer-centric experience quickly devolved once Scott made his purchase.

Every day since his first purchase, Scott's inbox has been filled with emails from Casper promoting other mattresses to buy. The problem, of course, is that Scott doesn't need a new mattress. The soonest he would need another mattress, barring any major issues, is seven years from now. Even though Casper owns all the data they need, they didn't take the time to understand Scott's context and stage in the buyer journey.

Rather than engaging Scott in a meaningful way, continuing to provide value and increase loyalty, they're treating him like an ATM, hoping to get more money out of him with little-to-no consideration for what else he might be interested in.

Does that sound familiar?

This is the exact strategy that many nonprofits have been using for years, despite dismal response rates and even worse donor retention data. The fundamental problem unresponsive nonprofit organizations share with Casper is that their singular focus is on achieving a monetary transaction.

Casper didn't consider that Scott would receive more value (and likely share more about his experience) if he were provided mattress care information or even bedroom decoration ideas instead of nonstop product promotion. Rather than continue the momentum of a perfectly great customer experience, Casper annoyed Scott so much that the only thing we heard in the office was how he would never need this many mattresses!

Imagine the negative experience a donor has when the only call-to-action you ever give them is to donate. As the organization supporting the cause that they care about most, it's disheartening that all your donors might hear at the end of the day is, "Give more. That last donation wasn't good enough."

For years, we've been involved with organizations who include a tear-off donation ask in every mail piece, including donation receipts. If you ask one of these organizations why they include a gift ask in the receipt itself, the response is predictably, "Because several donors give again on their receipt response device." In one sense, they are right. Asking everywhere, all the time appears to generate more gifts. But these nonprofits fail to appreciate the alienation experienced by the vast majority of donors who don't give again. While they are able to pick up a few additional donations in the short run, they rarely appreciate the long-term erosion of donor loyalty created by pushy, irrelevant marketing.

RESPONSIVE PLAY:
DISTRIBUTE LONGFORM CONTENT WITH ADS TO CREATE SUBJECT MATTER EXPERT DONORS

Donors want to advocate for your organization, but often they don't know how. The best way to grow generosity is to turn your biggest fans into your best fundraisers and advocates. Take steps to listen to your donors in order to find out who wants to be an influencer in their community. Then give them the tools to be successful. Here are a few plays to help you get started.

Execute

- Identify the content that is highly valuable to each of your donor personas that can also be easily created by your team. Find the areas of intersection and create longform content assets specifically targeted towards your most engaged donors. The best content leads with stories (preferably video) and backs up the stories with stats, history, etc.

- Create an automated email marketing campaign for your existing base that encourages the donor personas you've identified to download the content piece to take a deep dive into the area or program that interests them most. Send 1-3 emails in the campaign.

- Send email recipients to a customized landing page with a tracking pixel and a lead form to ensure that you have visibility into traffic, engagement, and conversion metrics.

- Add lead forms to content so that you learn something new even if the donor has engaged with your assets over many years. Always make sure that you use lead forms as an opportunity to learn a new piece of relevant information. Focus more on giving back to visitors rather than just asking for a gift.

- Make sure your lead form CTAs and messaging feel like exclusive opportunities to join your organization in the fight for the cause.

- Once you've educated your influencer audience, make them feel like superheroes! Give them ways to talk about their newfound role with your cause within their sphere of influence (sample social posts, playbooks for hosting local events, etc).

- Set up another automated email nurture sequence for donors who have downloaded your content piece to suggest next best actions. Ensure that donors receive suggestions that best fit their behavior. If this is a new person who hasn't donated yet, use the automated email series to send them to new, related content and finally a page to engage as an advocate along with giving page. If it is an existing donor you already know a lot about, suggest that they schedule a time to talk to one of your team members to find out what else they would love to see from your organization.

- Create Facebook, Twitter, and Instagram ads and promoted content to drive not-yet-engaged visitors to content. In many cases, recruiting advocates can be a better acquisition strategy than asking for gifts. Look for people who are active in your cause generally but aren't yet associated with your organization. Use Facebook targeting and lookalike audiences to refine your ad target.

- For all traffic that landed on your landing page but did not submit their information via a form, create promoted posts and social advertisements on Facebook and Instagram sending those individuals similar content or retarget them to get them back on the content landing page.

- Create a lookalike audience on Facebook from the converted donors and advocates and create an additional advertising campaign to push your content to new audiences.

- Update your strategy with new longform content pieces every quarter.

Suggest donors provide additional information at each conversion point to continue to build a deeper connection with more context about what motivates them.

The reason donors tell nonprofits that they're sending too much mail or email is because those messages aren't adding value. They treat donors like an ATM. Instead, relevant, contextual suggestions that are focused on driving donor value inspire loyalty. And they provide the trust and permission that nonprofits need to engage in frequent, two-way conversations about the cause.

KNOW WHEN AND WHAT TO ASK

In the past decade in America, we've faced a chaotic political climate. No matter which side you land on, it is becoming increasingly important to pay attention to policy decisions and current events. Because of our current environment, many policy organizations are ignoring response principles in favor of urgent, incendiary calls to action. If policy organizations were more focused on providing value, they would be constantly providing rich content to help constituents truly understand the issues and develop deep engagement. In a perfect world, these organizations would focus on providing engaging updates on policy, closing the loop on initiatives that they're currently pushing, or giving detailed information about candidates and issues based on your geographic location. The result would long-term momentum for their cause rather than unsustainable spikes in revenue.

Instead, many policy organizations have simply kept to the same strategy of leading with a bombastic headline and then asking for donations in every email send. It's exhausting, even for the most fired-up citizens. This approach can occasionally produce short-term results, but over the long run generosity begets generosity. Focusing on delivering value to constituents first — and then suggesting the best next step based on each person's level of engagement — will always produce more loyal donors who stick around beyond a one-time donation.

Responsive fundraisers don't abandon the call for donors to donate — that wouldn't do anyone any good. Instead, they ask for money for the *right* project exactly when they know it will resonate most. Responsive fundraisers are constantly pushing towards higher and more valuable moments of conversion, and they know that in this pursuit, timing is everything.

Once you've established trust with your donors by listening and connecting in personal ways, you have an opportunity to suggest giving options that are the best fit for each individual.

A few weeks back, I was preparing to speak at a conference in Denver. The talk covered the core tenets of The Responsive Framework. I knew that I'd be talking to a lot of partners and nonprofits who were already embracing the framework and I couldn't have been more excited.

Part of my preparation involved finding the right shirt to wear on stage. I browsed through a few of my favorite stores, but eventually gave up. The shipping quotes didn't fit my timeline and I decided that what I already had in my closet was completely fine.

Unlike my experience with my wife's boots, however, my experience with retargeting ads was different. The shirt that I'd considered the week before showed up in my browser windows and I was primed to buy it. When I was researching case studies for my talk, this shirt showed up right next to the research, taunting me. As I started to think about all the additional speaking opportunities that might pop up in the next few months, the shirt started to make more and more sense to me. In fact, the particular store where I was browsing was able to identify my engagement and actually sent me a print catalog in the mail two weeks later.

Finally, after seeing the shirt in various contexts throughout my day, each time becoming more and more relevant to my immediate future, I bought the shirt. And, for the record, my closet is better for it. The relevant, omnichannel approach of this retargeting campaign worked because the brand was listening, making connections and suggesting the right actions at the right time for me.

So what's the difference between the boots and the shirt?

Me. Can I really fault one company for missing the mark and another one for hitting it? Well, yes. And this is exactly how your donors feel. The brands that stand out, the nonprofits that cut through the fray, are the ones that make sense of the data from people who interact with them in order to make the right suggestions at the right times. Just like with the shirt, when the suggestion resonates, people will act.

RESPONSIVE PLAY:
CREATE IMPACT STORIES WITH MULTI-CHANNEL DISTRIBUTION

Impact stories are the heart of your nonprofit. They're how you bring each and every donor closer to your cause and the change you're making in the world. Unfortunately, fundraisers and communications teams don't always have access to these kinds of compelling stories. Here's how you can break down silos between teams and create a responsive strategy for your impact stories.

Execute

- Create a path for field workers to indicate an impact story they discovered so that all teams are notified of the opportunity.

- Use multiple channels to bring the impact story to life. Shoot videos, record audio files, take photos, scan handwritten journal entries, and create graphic assets that bring the story to life and pull the donors in closer. Remember, whenever you create one piece of content you should be creating five more. A video can be easily parlayed into a complimentary blog post, landing page, short form Facebook ad, etc.

- Reframe each impact story to be relevant to each of your donor personas. Make sure to include heartwarming quotes, undeniable statistics, and powerful imagery to make the impact story resonate with each donor persona.

- Build a marketing automation workflow that tells the story through multiple mediums to each of your donor personas. Send parts of the story via email, add some details to your social media feeds, post parts of the story to your blog and YouTube page, and create a powerful direct mail piece that tells the impact story. Space each touchpoint out to tell the story in the most impactful way over time.

- Add a relevant suggestion to the end of the impact story to move digital donors to a landing page where they can learn more about the story they just heard.

- Create a tracking pixel to get a detailed look at what donors landed on the page, from which channels, and what actions they took while on the landing page.

- Follow up the impact story marketing automation campaign with a report about which mediums resonated best with which donor personas and identify better ways to tell the subsequent impact stories.

RESPONSIVENESS IN FINANCIAL AND NON-FINANCIAL ASKS

Responsive fundraising approaches financial asks by looking at the whole picture and taking into account context, channel, and non-financial commitments.

In responsive fundraising, your financial suggestions should always consider context. In today's world, there's no reason you should be sending the same $50 a month donation "ask" to all of your constituents. Your financial suggestion should always consider capacity. It doesn't make sense to suggest a college student give a $10,000 gift to a capital campaign (unless you know they have the wealth to actually respond), nor does it make sense to suggest that at year-end, a major donor make a $100 monthly commitment.

Financial suggestions should also consider the channel the donor came in on (email, event, etc) and their particular passions. If a donor only ever visits pages on your website about water, and they only attend events related to building wells, then don't suggest a donation to buy malaria nets. As with my experience with my wife's boots, suggestions without context create frustration and disloyalty.

Suggestions shouldn't always be financial commitments either. In fact, they will convert more frequently if you provide opportunities to learn more through an article, video, or event, giving time by volunteering, or using their influence in their various communities to invite others to connect to your organization. Your donors are real humans with time, talent, intelligence, and social capital to offer. The more you embrace a holistic approach to your suggestions, the more your donors will feel like they are truly part of your cause. And donors who give their time, talent, and network will ultimately become the hands and feet of your new donor acquisition strategy.

Your suggestions are a response to what you know about the individual and what you know is the next right action to commit to your charity in a deeper way. Every suggestion must be dynamic and respond to what you learned as you listened and made connections with each donor. Responsive gift suggestions allow the donor to feel like they are receiving just as much value as the organization.

At its core, responsive fundraising acknowledges that everyone has unique value and something to give. Instead of generic asks that push everyone to do or give the same thing, tap into your audience's different talents and capabilities and let them add richer value to your cause.

RESPONSIVE PLAY:
NURTURE PLANNED GIVING CANDIDATES

Unfortunately, some of the most neglected donor segments are those who have been giving to you for a long time. Nonprofits see them as a guarantee and, therefore, do not spend resources bringing them closer to the impact. As an organization you have a responsibility to continue to nurture long-time givers and find ways they can engage. One of the biggest opportunities for long-time, aging donors is planned giving. Using predictive analytics to drive planned gift engagement can be a powerful tool to increase generosity.

Execute

- Segment potential planned givers by combining age information with donors who have given for at least 3 years.

- Create an email and direct mail series that spans a few weeks that provides information about planned giving programs, future planning, and other relevant information.

- Include suggestions for potential planned givers to take surveys and meet with individuals from your team to talk more about their desires for your programs in the future and what motivated them to give in the first place.

- Send impact stories and the ways in which their planned gift will move progress forward on the important initiatives the donor cares about.

- Invite planned givers to an event in their community and bring a personalized gift for them as a token of appreciation and acknowledgement of their generosity.

- Assign a call task at the end of your series to chat with the donor over the phone. This call should aim to add value to the donor by explaining planned giving. Provide resources for planned giving in general without pushing exclusively for your organization. Your generosity shouldn't be contingent on getting named in their will. This approach adds value, builds trust, and focuses on giving to the donor before you get anything.

CHAPTER 11:

RESPOND TO DONORS STRATEGICALLY

"Silent gratitude isn't much use to anyone."

– Gladys Bronwyn Stern

Since the first store opened in 1967, Trader Joe's employees have worked to uphold the title of America's Favorite Grocery Store. Not only does the company go out of its way to take care of the employees, but the leadership team encourages the employees to go out of their way to take care of customers.

Often, as a customer of Trader Joe's browsing the aisles, you will stumble upon a food you've never tried before or a version of your favorite food that you aren't sure whether or not to buy. Trader Joe's employees are all encouraged to try new food offerings so they can give you an honest opinion and a helpful suggestion. Each suggestion made by employees in the store is a quick calculation of what that person likes, what their objectives are (are they making Thanksgiving dinner or a quick weekday meal?) and what else they are going to incorporate into their meal. In a matter of seconds, Trader Joe's employees listen, make connections with their expert knowledge of the inventory, and give valuable suggestions to their customers.

The real payoff — and why Trader Joe's has created a cult-like following of customers and a community of employees who thoroughly enjoy their work — is when employees connect with customers for the second, third, or even one hundredth time. In the subsequent interactions, employees not only have deep knowledge of the store's inventory, but now they know what those customers like, what flavors they gravitate towards, and how well equipped they are to tackle complicated recipes. Their suggestions are deeper, more relevant, and powerful. By continuously cycling through The Responsive Framework, Trader Joe's locations across the country build communities of loyal advocates who wouldn't dream of shopping anywhere else.

Your nonprofit can cultivate the same commitment to your cause. It requires dedicating yourself to the process of The Responsive Framework and an empathetic understanding of all your donors, not just the few who give major gifts.

Sound crazy? Believe it or not, it's possible. And what's more, it works.

AUTHENTIC HUMAN CONNECTION

Your organization should combine the data and insights pulled from your various technology softwares and your expert knowledge from years of experience in the industry. While a tool can tell you it's time to suggest a new action and give you options, donors will always appreciate when they feel like the suggestion is coming from a human with their best interests at heart.

OneHope is a nonprofit organization that was able to live out its commitment to donors in a way that changed the growth trajectory of their organization. When Nicole Johansson started as the Vice President of Advancement, she identified a practice that the organization had that was invaluable for their team and their donors. She saw that unlike other organizations, who might have felt disconnected from donors, OneHope's team built a direct connection to the donors and their generosity.

Everyone at the organization, no matter which department they were in, had a responsibility to get on the phone with donors once a month. The only rule was: no asks could be made on the calls. Instead, employees were to have a real conversation with the donors. She saw her team get to know the people who were making the organization's work possible. She heard them talk about donors' hopes for the future, their interests, and the ways they were connected to the OneHope community. Most importantly, her team figured out ways that OneHope could better serve their donors. They could find out what donors needed more and less of, and discover new creative ways to build connections.

Like Trader Joe's employees, the OneHope team had the opportunity to listen, connect, and suggest in real time. Out of the monthly phone calls, friendships were born, new passions were ignited, and donors felt more deeply connected to OneHope because they knew the people behind every communication piece. The fact that the entire organization did it together only made the effects stronger. Soon, generosity was evolving into more meaningful and frequent acts of giving.

The biggest shift in responsive fundraising is letting go of the heavy reliance on donating as your only suggestion. Understand that modern donors expect the relationship they have with you to be a two-way street. If they don't see the value you're providing to them via beneficiary stories or community connections, they'll move on to another organization that does value them.

Jeremy Reis phrased it perfectly when he said,

> *Donors don't give to your organization, they give to make the world a better place. I hate to break it to you. Most of your donors (not all, but most) aren't giving to your organization. They're giving to change a life. To make the world a better place. To fight for a cause (or against one!). To save a life. They're giving because it makes them feel good. They're not giving because your organization itself is super cool. You are super cool, but it's the results (not just the work!) your donor is interested in. When you begin to forget that, you start talking about how tremendous your organization is. You start bragging about yourself. Stop doing that! Brag about your donor. Show her results. Tell her she's changing lives and saving people. Give her a reason to know her donation is being used effectively.* [38]

Make sure that your suggestions make sense for that individual donor. If you make an educated guess and suggest the wrong thing, listen for that immediate feedback so your next suggestion resonates. For example, if a donor exhibits engagement behaviors that suggest they are ready to give $100 more than their last

---

[38] Jeremy Reis, "*Raise More Money with Email: Activate Digital Giving at Your Nonprofit,*" Nonprofit Donor Press. August 8 2017.

donation, but when you made the suggestion they ignored you, don't be afraid to call the donor directly. Seek out the answers for donor behavior or interests you don't understand.

Don't use that time to overwhelm them with more communications trying to convince that person to donate. Instead, understand what you could do better to inspire the generosity that aligns with their hopes for the future. In some cases, you can automate a reminder to reach out to donors who disengage with your suggestions. Identify those in your team who can make donor calls, those who can send selfie vlogs via social channels, and those who can meet up with lapsed donors in person and create automated tasks when a donor has disengaged over a specific amount of time. Video emails tools like BombBomb and VidYard can be amazing tools to drive this type of personal connection with your team and solicit honest feedback. That way, you don't have to play catch up or waste time reminding people why they stopped responding.

Responsive fundraising allows your nonprofit to put processes, systems, and automation in place to be actively engaged in donor relationships. When it's working correctly, you should have full transparency into each individual donor's interests, motivations, and next best action. No matter how often those variables change, being responsive means you are set up to evolve your relationship alongside the donor instead of reacting to their unanticipated changes in behavior.

RESPONDING TO DONOR SIGNALS

A few years ago, Watsi, a nonprofit dedicated to providing healthcare to individuals in developing countries, launched an interesting initiative called Watsi's Universal Fund. It was a way for donors to give monthly to the organization. At the time, subscription startups were popping up all over the place adopting the "set-it-and-forget-it" payment options. Grace Garey, a Watsi co-founder, built a strategy where people could give as much (or as little) as they wanted to provide healthcare to people who needed it most.

When Watsi had the idea for the platform, they knew that they still had to find a way to provide monthly value to donors. Unlike their for-profit counterparts, a monthly subscription to a nonprofit didn't result in a fun surprise in your mailbox every month. There was a warm feeling some might get, but if Watsi didn't actively nurture that warm feeling, Grace and her team knew that they would lose donors.

What Grace and her team realized was that they could provide constant relevant value, even if it wasn't in a subscription box. "During this campaign, it became really critical for us to overcommunicate to people where there money was going," said Grace. "We spent a lot of time engineering a new type of monthly email that Universal Fund members get that reminds them that they are donating on a monthly basis, even if they aren't coming back to the site. We still introduce them to a patient benefiting from their support, and reassure them that they'll get a follow-up about their condition. Since we're not giving people something tangible, we need to make this reminder really impactful and clear."[39]

Each month, Watsi seized the opportunity to take what they had heard from their donors the previous month and apply their

---

39 "What Startups Can Learn from Watsi's Wildly Successful Email Campaign," First Round Review. https://firstround.com/review/what-startups-can-learn-from-watsis-wildly-successful-email-campaign/

learnings to make their email marketing more relevant, impactful, and more effective at compelling donors to take a second action. Watsi knew that this particular group of donors was already committed to recurring donations, so they didn't spend their time asking for another donation. Instead, they closed the loop by highlighting ways in which donors were helping the cause. They celebrated donors' generosity and provided content they could share with their families, friends, and communities that highlighted all the good they were doing in the world.

"We realized the closer we can bring people to the work we're doing on the ground — to the patient, to the hospital providing the care, to the person's family — the more they will feel like they are having a significant interaction, and that's the product we deliver for every donation," said Grace.

Responsive fundraisers must understand that their role is not just to increase revenue for their organization. Rather, to be an effective fundraiser to modern donors, you must know the right ways to keep their passion burning for your cause and create more good in the world. Where you might have had to guess the right answers before and relied on luck, responsive fundraisers acquire the tools and data they need so that they don't have to guess. They can rely on insights and the creativity of their team to find a suggestion that works.

RESPONSIVE PLAY:
CREATE MONTHLY ENGAGEMENT TASKS

We know that our subscription-based economy has resulted in more people signing up for recurring donations. It seems our entire lives are driven by monthly "as-a-service" products. Nonprofits have the ability to leverage this trend to create predictable, sustainable revenue from monthly donors. A recent study from *The State of Modern Philanthropy* tells us that recurring donors have a 42 percent higher lifetime value than their non-recurring counterparts.[40] What nonprofits haven't figured out is how to add value to donors month after month so they don't cancel their gift. Here are a few suggestions to make your organization more responsive to monthly givers.

Execute

- Schedule a monthly newsletter specifically for those who have signed up for monthly giving. Include information about the impact they have made in the last month as a result of their donation.

- Add tags for monthly givers when they pass milestones. Ensure that they never go more than 6 months without being celebrated in some way, whether that is a social media shout out, a special

---

40   Ellie Burke, "Just Released: The State of Modern Philanthropy 2018," Classy. https://www.classy.org/blog/the-state-modern-philanthropy-report/

email send, or a handwritten letter thanking them for their contribution.

- Create an end-of-year donor experience that provides insights into what was affected by their monthly gifts. Make sure to publish the experience on multiple media to ensure it resonates with each donor persona.

- Automate a donor call task for your team to call monthly givers every 9 months. Include any information that is learned through the conversation to the donor profile in your CRM.

- Identify engagement metrics that might indicate a desire to run a peer-to-peer fundraising campaign or advocate for your cause in another way. If donors exhibit those behaviors, enroll them in an automated advocacy recruitment workflow.

- Offer suggestions for new ways to give after their 1-year anniversary including event attendance, and volunteer work.

That's an important distinction between past behavior and future strategies. Remember, donors are more educated than they've ever been about the state of the world. The information surrounding the causes that your nonprofit supports can be found with a simple Google search on their iPhone. Donors can do everything from fact-check your information, ask their network if you're a trustworthy organization, or yell about your positive impact from the proverbial rooftops. A more informed donor base means a more engaged donor base.

In general, donors make emotional, relational decisions to give (and that's OK!). Then they look for rational proof to validate their decision. They can now get relational motivation from a community, emotional stories of impact, and data-based insights about your cause all without interacting directly with your organization. Ellinger described the predicament when he wrote in *The New Nonprofit*, "People view excessive or inappropriate communications (for them) as a waste of money and thus as a proxy for what their donation is really doing. If your letter says they bought a mosquito net and your behavior says they bought 20 direct mail letters, which one are they going to believe?" If you're listening, donors will tell you what they want from you, when, and why. All your organization must do is be responsive to their signals.

REACTIVE RESPONSE AND PROACTIVE RESPONSES

The Responsive Framework doesn't mean that your organization can't be proactive about inspiring action from donors, potential donors, and others in your network. In fact, there are two approaches you can use, one specifically designed for the times when you want to reach out first. Here's what I mean.

Reactive responsive fundraising is just what you might expect: you use donor input as the basis for your outreach strategy. Your organization outlines what you know about the donor, considers what else you could learn, and combines that with their most recent action to create an engagement strategy. Reactive fundraising typically includes responding to gifts, event attendance, email opens, web visits, etc. in real-time when the action takes place.

For example, imagine a new person donates $500 to your organization. The first action your organization should take is to acknowledge their generosity and express gratitude. So, you send a thank-you email.

Hallie,

Wow! Thank you for your donation. $500 is enough to buy all the equipment we need to provide a clean water well in Uganda. With your help, 200 people outside of Kitgum will have improved health and quality of life, no longer having to travel hours for water.

We are incredibly grateful you chose to give today and can't wait to learn more about what else you're passionate about. Keep an eye out for updates from our field team about the impact your generosity has made. In the meantime, you can check out our YouTube channel to see the incredible Ugandans people like you have helped in the past!

We also have a great ebook designed to help educate our supporters about the water crisis and find other, non-financial ways that you can engage in the cause.

Download the Free eBook here.

Thank you again,

Sam

You've directly responded to Hallie's action and set yourself up for a few learning opportunities without asking for more money from her. You've provided her with entertaining videos, transparency around her impact, and a personal contact at your organization, should she want to reach out about doing more. You've also given back to her in tangible ways and invited her to participate more holistically in the cause.

Depending on Hallie's actions, you can follow up in two weeks with personal stories from beneficiaries, social media initiatives she can share or information about your process of building new wells. If you've focused on delivering value to Hallie, she's far more likely to share her stories about her new passions in conversations with friends. Based on Hallie's behavior after your first email, automatic next steps might include:

- If she has a big Twitter following, she could be sent a series of emails that explain how to enroll in a peer-to-peer fundraising program.

- If she clicks on content in the email she could be sent two more emails over the next week with similar content.

- If she gives again in the next 60 days she could get a phone call to thank her plus answers to all her questions about the organization, the cause, and your different programs.

- If there's an update from the fields related to the project she gave to (i.e. progress on the well), that update should automatically be emailed to her. Closing the loop on generosity gives donors a tangible result to share with their closest friends.

Each of Hallie's choices informs the next response from your nonprofit. The best part is, that response can be created and sent automatically using marketing automation so she is never left without a path to follow.

Proactive responses are slightly different in that they rely on sophisticated donor profiles. Your organization uses what you've learned from past donors to build comprehensive, responsive engagement tracks based on their most likely behaviors.

Let's say you are fundraising for a college and a current donor, Conor, introduces you to another alumnus, Jess, at the first tailgate of the season. You have Jess' contact information, but she's never engaged with your communications, let alone donated. She's part of a contact list that (at the moment) you have no plan for.

However, you do know that Conor is very close to Jess and can provide a few details about her interests, her career, and her best memories at your university. After a quick conversation with Conor, you realize that Jess fits your Uninspired Alumnus donor profile. You've been running an engagement campaign for this group for over a year and earned a 70 percent conversion rate.

Now, you can enroll Jess into your engagement campaign knowing there is a 70 percent chance she'll give. The first time Jess engages in a meaningful way (with email opens or clicks, shares or responses) you can transition into a mix of reactive responses and proactive responses. The point is to follow wherever the modern donor leads so that you can inspire generosity in an authentic, actionable way.

You can also gauge Conor's interest in helping you build a relationship with Jess outside of your campaign. So, you have a proactive way to nurture Jess back into the donor journey by providing materials you have verified people like her care about. You also have the opportunity to tag Conor as an "advocate" and enroll him in a marketing automation series of emails, social media engagements, and handwritten notes designed to help him tell your story to more people like Jess in his network.

Remember, Suggest is the phase of The Responsive Framework where your team can be most effective in terms of donor relationships and revenue growth. Each marketing automation task, call-to-action, and engagement strategy is built on data pulled directly from your donors. Every time you move through the Listen and Connect phase into the Suggest phase, you are learning exactly what you need to do in order to inspire the right action from your donors.

You will no longer be tied to a mass-marketing approach. You'll be equipped with the right information you need to suggest the right thing to each individual donor at the right time. If, at any point, you feel pulled to default into fundraising strategies that have always been done, push yourself through the Listen and Connect phase first. The information may reveal that the right answer is a direct mail piece to every donor on your list. But more than likely, as you recommit to Listen and Connect, your Suggest step will be a more meaningful, personalized action that your donors will do more often (and with more passion).

CHAPTER 12:

CASE STUDIES: THE RESPONSIVE FRAMEWORK IN ACTION

"Strategy without tactics is the slowest route to victory. Tactics without strategy is the noise before defeat."

– Sun Tzu

To understand the different ways The Responsive Framework can be incorporated into your nonprofit operations, I've created two case studies for you. I'll walk you through the different ways each organization exemplified responsive fundraising, plus point out a few extra steps that might have been helpful.

My hope is that you will use these case studies to inspire a list of ways your organization can implement personalized, automated engagements with your donor. If you'd like more responsive fundraising plays, we've put together a resource guide on our website. Download The Responsive Fundraising Playbook at virtuouscrm.com/responsive.

THE LAST WELL'S HOPE FLOATS INITIATIVE

The Last Well is a nonprofit started in 2008 by a group at Frontline Church in Washington D.C. Todd Phillips, the pastor at the church, was very passionate about serving the world's most vulnerable people. The Last Well decided to focus on Liberia, identifying it as the most challenging place in the world with the greatest need.

The founders of The Last Well created a simple mission they could work towards: "To provide access to safe drinking water for the entire nation of Liberia, border to border, and offer the gospel to every community we serve, by 2020."

In 2018, Todd knew that The Last Well had to start pushing themselves if they wanted to fulfill their mission. Despite providing access to clean water for 1.7 million Liberians, there were still 3 million people to serve. So Todd came up with an idea: The Hope Floats Initiative.

The plan was simple. Todd would live on a barge in Lake Ray Hubbard, just outside of Dallas, Texas, until he raised $2.29 million for The Last Well. He picked the location because it was in clear view of any drivers going east on Interstate 30. The plan was to use the 20-by-22-foot floating home to grab the attention of those driving by and hopefully turn that attention into donations.[41]

Todd also brought along his computer, a generator, and some lights he could use to share live video to The Last Well's Facebook feed.

---

41 Dana Branham, "After weeks afloat on Lake Ray Hubbard, fundraiser reaches goal of $2.3 million to help Liberians," The Dallas Morning News, November 6, 2018. https://www.dallasnews.com/news/2018/11/06/after-weeks-afloat-on-lake-ray-hubbard-fundraiser-reaches-goal-of-2-3-million-to-help-liberians/

Every day, he would update followers on what he was doing, how close they were getting to the fundraising goal, and simply talk about his experience.

Before he got on the barge, Todd hoped that he could reach the $2.29 million goal by the end of the week. Unfortunately, The Hope Floats Initiative extended over four weeks.

One particularly dangerous night, Dallas experienced record-setting rainfall and powerful storms. Family, friends, and supporters flooded Julie Phillips' phone with questions about Todd's health and safety. Julie thought that it might be a good idea to send everyone to the Facebook feed to get real-time updates directly from Todd. That's when things started to shift.

The nightly live streams started to attract more viewers and donations as people started to share with their communities. Eventually, one local business owner decided to donate the last bit of money needed for The Last Well to reach their goal, officially ending The Hope Floats project.

Todd, elated to reach his goal (and get off the boat), invited everyone in their Facebook community to a local restaurant to celebrate the fundraising goal and the fact that thousands of Liberians would get access to clean, safe drinking water.

Responsive Framework Tactics at Play

Let's dissect what is responsive about The Last Well's Hope Floats Initiative.

First, Julie's decision to point people directly to the Facebook page was responsive and incredibly valuable to the project as a whole.

It gave donors a single place to go for all the information that was relevant to them. They could engage in the project in real-time, and didn't have to wait for a response or an update. It gave them a way to be actively involved in the fundraising.

The nightly live events that Todd held on the barge also allowed for donors to immerse themselves in the project itself. The chats that were born out of the live event also allowed Todd to connect with newcomers and suggest actions for those who wanted to get involved.

Finally, the celebration dinner at the end of the initiative was a way to close the loop with donors. It brought them into the celebration and let them meet others in the community offline that they'd been engaging with online for a month.

It was certainly a successful project with elements of The Responsive Framework. But, now that you know the details of a successful responsive framework, I'm sure you can see some additional opportunities where The Last Well could have implemented The Responsive Framework even further.

Potential Additional Responsive Framework Tactics

The first opportunity to employ responsive fundraising that sticks out to me is the launch of the project. As the story is told, Todd thought of the idea himself as a way to raise awareness. He identified the fundraising goal and the timeline without consulting the donors or his local community. In The Responsive Framework, donors to The Last Well might have signaled how much they were willing to give or, better yet, pledged their commitment to raise awareness for the event in order to amplify the message even more. Donors who are included in the creation of a campaign consistently feel more ownership in its success. Remember, donors want to feel like they are *part* of the cause and with a pre-engaged group of donors Todd might have hit his goal a little quicker with slightly less sea sickness.

Confining his nightly updates to Facebook may have also been a missed opportunity. While there are billions of users on Facebook, it is still not everyone's preferred communication style, especially between individuals and their favorite nonprofits. A responsive nonprofit might try these additional tactics to include more donors in The Hope Floats Initiative:

- Three weeks prior to the campaign launch, they could have sent a preview email to their most loyal donors, and asked for feedback, ideas, and buy-in. This would have generated an early wave (pun intended) of support to help amplify the campaign.

- They could have segmented Dallas donors and sent a personalized email inviting them to come to Lake Ray Hubbard for a day of community. The Last Well might have suggested each donor with more than 300 Facebook friends to bring someone who hasn't heard of The Last Well to see what they are all about.

- They might have automated an email sequence that sends a recap of each Facebook livestream to all donors who aren't currently Facebook fans of The Last Well, encouraging them to watch the video and become a fan to be part of the community.

- Pull a list of the most engaged Facebook commenters on the livestream events to create tasks to call them at the end of the week, thanking them for their generosity, time and asking what they care about most as a donor of The Last Well.

- Create automated email series that sends to all donors celebrating fundraising milestones. Use the opportunity to suggest they follow the journey on social media, share the idea with their friends, or donate again.

- Create an automated workflow for anyone that donated to the campaign, which included emails over the course of 1-2 weeks thanking them and suggesting ways they can amplify the campaign outside of giving, including emailing the live feed to friends and family, sharing a promo video on Instagram or Facebook, and even distributing promotional fliers within their local coffee shops and gathering places.

- Publish a giving page on their Facebook feed, specific to The Hope Floats Initiative. Make the giving page a data-driven page that suggests giving amounts based on donor behavior.

- Test different livestream times to engage audiences in different timezones. Include some of the employees in Liberia in the livestream to pull donors closer to the cause and inspire generosity.

- Republish livestream clips on Instagram, Twitter and other outlets to increase sharing.

Of course, each day the project is happening, donors are providing more signals and giving The Last Well more ways to connect and suggest.

Just to be clear, none of these points are intended to be a critique. The Hope Floats Initiative is one of the most innovative examples of responsive fundraising I've heard. The Last Well absolutely crushed it! Also, they may have executed on a few of these suggestions in ways that we never saw or appreciated. But hopefully these suggestions help spur your imagination for how you might implement similar responsive tactics.

Post-Event Opportunities for the Future of The Hope Floats Initiative

Another function of The Responsive Framework is that it allows your nonprofit to create connections between every project, program, and fundraising initiative to inspire future acts of giving. As you Listen, Connect, and Suggest, you're also iterating on ideas and making them more meaningful, relevant, and impactful to your donors. Here are some ideas that The Last Well could use once The Hope Floats Initiative ended to ensure that generosity continues.

- Post to Facebook inviting new Facebook followers to subscribe to their email list using a trackable link. Enroll all new subscribers from Facebook into a personalized email workflow that welcomes them to The Last Well, providing new ways to engage that weren't discussed on Todd's livestreams.

- Send a postcard via direct mail to all engaged Facebook donors. Include a handwritten thank you from the entire team and a link to see images of the wells that were built thanks to their generosity. Track users to that webpage to understand who responds to direct-mail.

- Send a survey via email to all donors who gave during The Hope Floats Initiative asking where Todd should go during the next Hope Floats Fundraising event.

- Identify donors primed for a peer-to-peer campaign, send them an invitation to learn more about how they can build their own barge (or maybe something slightly less dangerous!) and run their own Hope Floats Initiative.

- Create an automated email marketing campaign that recaps the entire project to those who did not engage with any of The Hope Floats Initiative communications. Provide information about the fundraising success, ask for signals that might indicate why they did not feel compelled by the event, and use their answers to brainstorm new ways to bring these donors into the organization.

- Build landing pages that provide information about all wells that were built thanks to donors of The Hope Floats Initiative. A/B test the landing page to lead with statistical information or beneficiary stories. Use website behavioral data to understand what resonates with donors most.

- Leverage Facebook's advertising to sponsor posts on the anniversary of The Hope Floats Initiative to users who were engaged during the first year, providing information about progress and the newest goal needed to complete The Last Well's mission in 2020.

As donors engage with each communication, The Last Well can understand what their donors care about, how they want to learn about the progress and when the right time to suggest an act of generosity is. With more robust behavior data at their disposal, The Last Well will be able to host more responsive fundraising events and hopefully accomplish their mission.

THE SICKKIDS VS CAMPAIGN

In 2018, The SickKids Foundation had a single goal: to raise enough money to build a new hospital. The way they saw it, twenty-first-century medicine shouldn't be held back by a facility built in 1949. Modern medicine necessary to cure progressive illnesses required a modern building. They needed bigger hallways, adaptable rooms and comfortable beds to accommodate families staying at The Hospital for Sick Children over long periods of time.

Normally, The SickKids Foundation raised $150 million annually. That was enough to keep the facility running and serving the sick children throughout Canada. However, in order to reach their goal of building a world-class facility that the children deserved, they needed to raise $1.3 billion.

That kind of fundraising increase is difficult under any circumstances. It's almost impossible during the generosity crisis nonprofits are experiencing. But, as an organization focused on innovation, The SickKids Foundation leaned on responsive principles to give them the right path forward.

What they found was their core demographic, moms in their mid-forties, were consistently giving no matter the circumstances. The women who were connected to The SickKids Foundation were loyal and dedicated to the cause. What the data also illuminated was that SickKids had a problem similar to The American Cancer Society example shared earlier in this book: men were missing from the core donor demographic. More perilous, the data also showed that when men did give, they tended to give more. So The SickKids Foundation knew they needed a strategy to bring men closer to the cause.

What they created was the SickKids VS campaign. The campaign included a multi-channel, multi-media approach, but the core of the campaign was a new set of SickKid videos. The video campaign shifted the way that the organization presented the issue of illness. Instead of heartwarming videos of survival, the videos portrayed a strong, happy child supported by an entire community. They invited donors to be part of the fight, to engage in action and take control of the illness that affected their kids and other kids in their community. They knew from their constituents that it was unfair to expect a child to somehow "fight" cancer on their own. Instead of expecting kids to fight cancer, they reframed the narrative to be SickKids (and its donors) fighting cancer on behalf of the kids. The video campaign created a buzz that The SickKids Foundation hadn't experienced in years, and the fundraising was through the roof. Over 740,000 donors gave, with a total of 100,000 monthly donors. In a single year, The SickKids Foundation raised $159 million, with $2.2 million raised in a single day event.[42]

As part of the series, SickKids also began to identify tribes of constituents. One video featured a "Join Your Crew" message that

---

42 Annual Report 2018-2019, SickKids. http://web.sickkidsfoundation.com/
    annual-report-2018/

encouraged chefs, barbers, techies and even dog people to join the fight. SickKids understood that giving works best when it's supported by a network, so they empowered related tribes to stand together in battle.

The project is not over. In fact, even though it was the most successful fundraising year, there is still a long way to go. But, as they said in their video at the beginning of 2019, they have created the necessary momentum to build a new hospital for Canada's children.

Responsive Framework Tactics in Play

The SickKids VS campaign was a comprehensive campaign that included merchandise sales, traditional marketing tactics, and media coverage that helped spread the goal of the campaign. While we don't have insights into every responsive tactic they used, here are some we can identify immediately.

- By identifying their core donor demographic, The SickKids Foundation was able to remove them from the fundraising data to understand how much other donors were giving. Listening to each persona segmentation allowed for the necessary brainstorming to connect to new donors.

- Incorporating different CTAs in their VS campaign, The SickKids Foundation was able to reach different donors at different times. They could suggest the purchase of merchandise, attendance to an event, a stay at AirBnb, a traditional donation, video view or engagement with Olympians, celebrities and other donors who were engaged in the VS campaign. That diversity contributed to increased generosity from donors.

- They used video engagement data to inform the newest installments in the SickKids VS video campaign. By understanding which videos inspired more donations, shares, comments and views, The SickKids Foundation could create better, more relevant videos as the campaign aged, making it more and more powerful for donors.

- They published an annual report that highlighted all the major successes from the year. This tactic closed the loop for donors, proved transparency on the part of the Foundation and improved trust — all necessary factors in donor retention and increased generosity.

- They created a line of merchandise that allowed donors to define their communities, bringing each individual closer to the cause as well as closer to the group of likeminded donors that lived in their communities.

We can safely assume that there were also email marketing tactics, donor phone calls, and direct mail sends included throughout the year of the campaign. And the whole of these tactics led to an incredibly impactful responsive fundraising campaign along with a record-breaking fundraising year.

Potential Additional Responsive Framework Tactics for SickKids

Here are just a few of the additional initiatives that SickKids could have used in their efforts. As with The Last Well, many of these were likely employed in some form by SickKids but hopefully the list of suggestions inspires ideas.

- Incorporate different storytelling channels based on donor behavior. Use audio content, photo galleries, blogs and journal entries to tell the story for those who don't respond as strongly to video content.

- Create an episodic video campaign that highlighted the children the donors were rallying around in order to bring them closer and understand which stories drive more donations from their newly-engaged male donors and their loyal female donors.

- Leverage the video descriptions to suggest different actions for viewers to take. Test different CTAs to understand what donors are most likely to do after watching a video. For example, do they want to know more about the foundation? Send them to an about page or video. Do they want to donate immediately? Send them to a giving page with data-driven suggestions for donation amounts. Do they want to share with their network? Give them a scripted tweet to share with their network.

- Survey new donors to understand what about the new building is important to them. Pull insights from the responses to launch a secondary fundraising campaign that connects donors directly to the progress of the new hospital build.

- Aggregate the names of people who viewed, shared, and engaged with the videos across all social media channels to set up a retargeting ad campaign that pushes people to the donate page. Use website behavior data to understand the new donors the video campaign is attracting on a deeper level.

- Survey loyal donors for ideas about the newest VS video ideas. Use their stories of success to show how donors have a direct impact on their fellow Canadians.

The Responsive Framework has the biggest impact when you use it on all channels for all donors. There will be modifications and iterations for each of your donor personas, but having a plan for every possible donor signal is the best way to ensure that you will reach your fundraising goals and improve your donor relationships.

Opportunities for the Future SickKids VS Campaign

The SickKids Foundation understands that the work cannot stop simply because the year is over. The Responsive Framework demands that they continue to learn and work on their donor engagements. Here are some ideas that could be used to extend the momentum of their successful campaign.

- Create a landing page that shows the fundraising goals for building a new hospital along with donor stories. Add a fundraising form to the landing page that populates variable generosity suggestions based on the previous giving data of each website visitor.

- Build an automated workflow that sends the existing SickKids VS videos to new donors, explaining the success of their 2018 fundraising efforts and inviting them to be part of the movement.

- Make it possible for donors to create their own VS merchandise with the names of kids who were positively impacted by SickKids. Merchandise could be purchased at donor-led events in the community or by families who have benefited from the Hospital for Sick Children.

- Create a peer-to-peer campaign where donors can sponsor families or rooms based on the illness they want to fight against.

- Make phone calls to donors asking how their family has been impacted and what illnesses they're most interested in fighting. Connect donors in the same communities with those who are fighting the same illnesses. Encourage them to spread the word in their neighborhoods in order to build the new facility faster.

- Facilitate hand-written letters from the families who benefited from the generosity of donors. Letters could be written once and then copied for wide distribution. Print a trackable link on each letter to understand which donors are most compelled to action right after receiving mail from your organization.

- Use an ad campaign on social media that features Canadian media personalities to understand the interests of donors. Use that information to create new videos that highlight music, sports, gamers or other hobbies.

The responsive fundraising tactics will look different for your organization, and likely, for each campaign your organization runs. However, one thing remains true: if you set up each engagement in a way that allows you to Listen, Connect and Suggest, you will see more generosity from your donors. You will see more loyalty, more advocacy and deeper connections. That's how you overcome a generosity crisis and keep yourself connected to your donor base for decades to come.

CHAPTER 13:

HOW TO EVOLVE YOUR ORGANIZATION TO ADOPT THE RESPONSIVE FRAMEWORK

"Resources will tend to flow naturally toward you when you focus on the most important aspect of the fund-raising process: creating human connections."

— Jennifer McCrea, The Generosity Network

The Gathering is an annual event that brings together some of the best minds in the nonprofit space to talk about the future of generosity. Unlike other conferences that happen every year, The Gathering's main focus is to facilitate conversations that help people talk through ideas, listen, and learn. It started as a simple meeting between friends — a modern-day version of the Jeffersonian Dinner. Now, multiple keynote speakers present during The Gathering, but largely, the value is still in the conversations that happen between speeches.

The first year I was blessed with an invitation to The Gathering, I remember observing how large donors took the initiative to solve problems they knew nonprofits didn't have the time or space to solve. They shared information about where they were giving, how they were giving, and brainstormed ways they could all be more effective with their generosity.

These were people who had lived innovation in their everyday corporate lives for decades. The fact that some nonprofits didn't meet their expectations wasn't going to stop them from doing the good they wanted to see in the world.

Two important revelations hit me at that moment. The first was the truth behind the old adage, "If you don't do it, someone else will." I watched as individual donors collaborated to solve problems that were important to them despite the fact that their primary role wasn't to run a nonprofit. That passion and proactive approach to their own experience is reflected in every single one of your donors.

The second revelation was how rarely I observe the same proactive, collaborative, and creative sessions within nonprofit teams or between related nonprofits. It makes sense that nonprofit team members have a difficult time collaborating. With such high stakes, each person must have the singular focus of doing their job efficiently. Most employees don't feel like they have time to check in with the progress of other departments or bother their coworkers with a new idea that could be innovative for the organization. The result is siloed individuals doing siloed work at the expense of your donors and beneficiaries.

Silos that may have been constructed out of necessity in the early days of your operation are actively hurting it now that you've grown and donors have evolved. It's time that you evolve with them. The essential shifts your nonprofit must make in order to successfully implement The Responsive Framework your fundraisers so desperately need, start at the top. Leadership in each department must not only understand The Responsive Framework and commit to working through it, but they must also model the collaborative nature of The Responsive Framework to their internal teams.

Each directive or benchmark you deliver to the individuals at your nonprofit must also be accompanied by an invitation to iterate and improve the idea using what they know about your donors' motivations and the work of the rest of your organization. The only way to progress is when everyone is working together. It may seem like common sense, but it isn't the norm right now.

Many of the nonprofits we work with have a massive, unspoken wall between their fundraising, communication, and program teams. The communications team provides updates on what the organization is doing, the fundraising team works with donors, and the program team does that "real" work of the nonprofit. Occasionally, communications will ask program for an update on the work or fundraising will have input in a direct response email from communications but, largely, these departments operate in their own siloes.

This approach was tolerable in an era when donors had fewer choices and were more willing to blindly trust nonprofits without transparency or connection to the cause. But, in our hyper-connected world, donors are bombarded with thousands of marketing messages and they are experiencing increased demands on their time and money. In this quagmire of information and ads, it is almost impossible to determine who to follow or trust.

Imagine the extra layer of confusion and mistrust your donors feel when they get a variety of information and CTAs from different teams in your nonprofit. It's inefficient, ineffective, and distracting from the real issue: doing good in the world.

To address this problem, it is critical that your communications department is working daily with fundraising to personalize communications and build trust. Modern donors expect a single conversation across all channels whether it comes from your communications or marketing team. In the for-profit world, the term "smarketing" has emerged to describe the combination of sales and marketing to provide a singular customer experience. The same can be said for nonprofits. We need "commraising" (or "fundication") departments committed to a consistent donor experience.

It's also imperative that the program team work shoulder-to-shoulder with other teams to report on impact, tell stories, admit failure, and drive transparent change. More than anything, the program department at nonprofits must embrace the fact that donors aren't a means to an end. Healthy program teams see donors as part and parcel to the cause itself — and they feel a responsibility to bring donors in close to the good they are accomplishing in the world.

If you find yourself stuck on how you can encourage or facilitate collaboration with your internal teams, start with these changes to your structure. Other nonprofits have already found success using these models as their template to create new, innovative teams focused on responsive fundraising and donor relationships.

DEVELOPMENT AND COMMUNICATIONS TEAMS WORKING TOGETHER

Responsive nonprofits have a single goal in mind: put the donor at the center of everything. All the work that an organization does is a direct result of donors' generosity. The responsive nonprofit knows that they are simply the messenger between donors and beneficiaries.

This shift in focus has led many nonprofit operations to blend their development and communications teams. The benefit is a cohesive, comprehensive donor experience. Whether the person is a new subscriber or a long-time donor, the information shared between the communications and development teams provides a better, more holistic experience.

Many teams identify one person or a small group to oversee details of each donor across their departments in order to connect them with the right message at the right time. Using details about social capital, engagement, and data around donor motivations, a blended team can create new targeted development campaigns with better ROI. The investment in cohesive approaches to development, communications, and fundraising gives each donor a unique experience relevant to their interests resulting in higher lifetime value.

COMMUNICATIONS AND OPERATIONS/IT SUPPORTING EACH OTHER

Communications teams at responsive nonprofits need powerful software that can maintain the personalized experiences that constituents expect. With a tech-savvy member of your communications team, your nonprofit operations can streamline workflow, automate daily tasks, and give your team the freedom it needs to strategize around better donor relationships.

It's such an effective collaboration, in fact, that CMOs are now spending more of their budget on tech investments than IT departments.[43] Some are spending more on powerful software solutions than they are on talent. That's not the right solution for everyone, but it does show the impact the right tools can have on your nonprofit operations.

Instead of adding more and more people to scale simple tasks like sending thank you notes to online donors, your team can create a variety of notes and automate them to send whenever a donation is made. In collaboration with the IT team, communications professionals can identify points in their workflow that can be optimized, automated, or removed in favor of a more efficient responsive fundraising process. This approach requires IT and Operations teams who are fully committed to the responsive goals of other teams. Instead of seeing themselves as a gatekeeper, IT departments at nonprofits must shift to viewing themselves as an agile, offensive weapon to grow generosity.

PROGRAMS AND COMMUNICATIONS CROSSOVER

Donor-centric nonprofits prioritize the donor's involvement in the cause. Communications teams are starting to see how hungry donors are for content that closes the loop and highlights the impact they are making on the causes that are most important to

---

43   Chris Pemberton, "8 Top Findings in Gartner CMO Spend Survey 2018-19," Gartner, November 5, 2018 https://www.gartner.com/en/marketing/insights/articles/8-top-findings-in-gartner-cmo-spend-survey-2018-19

them. They're also seeing the timeline between communications shrink. They need more information in a variety of ways to ensure each donor feels a personal, relational connection to the impact of the organization.

It makes sense that communications teams are integrating with programs teams to create the content donors want. With regular communication and collaboration, nonprofits are publishing more content on a variety of channels using a handful of popular mediums. You can see photos, vlogs, sit-down conversations, personal letters, handwritten notes and infographics pop up in communications online and off. And donors appreciate it. No longer are they limited to a single newsletter about a cause that is important to them. They can engage in new ways that resonate most with them and inspire them to share.

NEW MARKETING TEAMS

Above all, the biggest change to nonprofit operations is a new structure for marketing teams. For years, nonprofits felt that marketing their work was in poor taste. The word "marketing" has been shunned by many nonprofits and even "fundraising" is treated like a necessary evil to accomplish the "real" work of the cause. What responsive nonprofits have realized is that good marketing practices are at the very core of creating a movement, telling your story, and creating more good. They've also realized that great marketing can't be done in a vacuum. It requires managing conversations across program, fundraising, and generating conversations with your donors and about your cause in general.

In past generations, people consumed marketing messages from a variety of businesses. Maybe one in every twenty TV commercials resonated with them. So, they trained themselves to look for those commercials they actually enjoyed and ignore everything else. In today's world, where everyone's life is curated with only the things they love, they pay attention to everything. It's estimated that the average consumer sees more than 5,000 ad messages per day.[44] But modern consumers and donors have changed their habits to rely on curated networks, newsfeeds, or Instagram personalities to get hyper-relevant, trusted information. To stand out against that kind of competition, nonprofits must evolve their marketing strategies. It's time to build a marketing team committed to moving from mass-blast communication to personalized, relationship-first marketing.

In many sectors within the nonprofit ecosystem, we're now seeing long-form, contiguous storytelling across multiple channels based on donor interest. Nonprofits are creating more touchpoints before the first donation ask. They are responding to the signals that the modern donors are sending, and they're seeing their fundraising start to improve as a result.

As your organization starts to work as a single entity, instead of fractured parts, your donors will start to have a comprehensive, deep understanding of who you are, what you value, and the trustworthy ways in which you impact the world. The fact is, people often derive some self-esteem from the brands they support, including your nonprofit. The more you act as a single entity, a single responsive experience, the more they will trust you and value the connection they have to you.

---

44   https://sjinsights.net/2014/09/29/new-research-sheds-light-on-daily-ad-exposures/

For example, let's say a prospective donor has recently learned about the human trafficking crisis from one of their friends. They watch a video story that brings them to tears and they feel desperate to fix the problem. Your new prospect wants to make a difference so they give $250. At the point they donate, they feel like they have a real vested interest in your cause. They feel like they are actually joining the fight against human trafficking (because they are!). Their heart is wrapped around their $250 donation and what they want it to accomplish. They are committed to being part of your cause not just a donor to the cause.

The charity on the other hand has a very different experience. Most employees of nonprofits have very little visibility into the fundraising process. There are typically a small handful of staff who have been tasked with communicating with donors and meeting the monthly budget needs. The two or three staff members who see the $250 gift are often completely relationally and emotionally disconnected from the giver. The donor goes into a sausage grinding process of receipt generation and is added to a direct mail list. Much of the communication they receive from the organization lacks the relational and emotional connection that they expected when they donated. Soon, their passion wanes for your organization. Even if they keep giving, their true gifts and passions often lay dormant and they are never truly drafted into the cause.

So what's the breakdown?

The culture of the organization doesn't value generosity. They aren't responding to the generous community despite the very passionate engagement from donors. Instead, they see donors as a means to an end.

Even if organizations do truly want to connect with donors relationally, they don't have the staff and resources to build thousands of personal relationships with their donors. And many are too afraid to take a risk and implement technological solutions and software that could help them make drastic, positive change.

In my experience, I've noticed three simple actions that organizations can take to begin shifting culture and building real authentic donor relationships in a cost-effective manner. I believe that these tactics can be invaluable in shifting your thinking about generosity and dramatically increasing your impact.

EQUIP YOUR TEAM WITH TOOLS

Digital literacy is not confined to Millennials and Gen Z. Smartphones have saturated every generation, but older generations are adopting technologies like tablets, laptops and computers.[45] We've covered how that affects your donors, but it's important to recognize the way it's affecting your employees.

Your employees, especially the younger ones who are executing the daily tasks, are accustomed to powerful, efficient software as a standard. Unfortunately, many nonprofits are beholden to outdated software that isn't suitable for the demands of modern donors. In an industry that is plagued with terribly high burnout rate, providing adequate software to your employees is just good business.

---

45 https://www.pewresearch.org/fact-tank/2019/09/09/us-generations-technology-use/

Consider your current suite of tools and take an honest assessment of the value they provide. Remember, The Responsive Framework will revolutionize the way your team collaborates and fundraises. Do you have the necessary tools to do that correctly?

Don't be afraid to get your team involved in the vetting process. Ask them what they need to be responsive. Chances are they know exactly what features they need from a reporting tool, a CRM, an email marketing platform, and a social listening tool. In fact, you might find that some of your employees have purchased solutions on their own. I've spoken to quite a few professionals who saw the added cost of a software solution to be worth it if it lowered their daily frustrations and improved efficiency.

EMBRACE FAILURE

If there's one thing that nonprofits can learn from their for-profit counterparts it is to embrace failure. This idea is much easier to welcome when you're using The Responsive Framework. In the past, when relationships with donors were based on nothing more than transactions, failure was much more detrimental to the future of your organization. In The Responsive Framework, your donors have a trusting, personal relationship with your organization and the decisions you make. They know that if a campaign fails or you make a choice that doesn't work out the way you hoped, your intentions are in the right place.

With that trust and open lines of direct communication, you can start to take chances to grow your nonprofit instead of simply maintain. I mentioned at the beginning of this book that people are only getting more generous, starting with Millennials. The reason you're not reaching them is because you aren't making the bold choices necessary to stand out to your donors.

Earlier in the book, I talked about how my friend Jon Burgess has been a champion for this concept at both Compassion International and David C Cook. I'll quote Jon again here because I think his insights are so critical for modern nonprofits.

> *Think it is absolutely crucial to create a culture where it's okay to fail. What we say in American business, not just nonprofits, is that we want you to be innovative, but we want all of your ideas to work. What happens is that you create this mentality of mediocrity, because the only ideas that see the light of day are those ideas where everybody can agree that there's some value there.*

In other words, innovation requires failure. Read any biography of great innovators, from the Wright Brothers to Elon Musk, and you'll find a path littered with failures and lessons learned.

In our section on building trust I also talked about Chris Horst and Peter Greer at Hope International. Chris and Peter have been at the cutting edge of fostering transparency and admitting failure publicly (event to donors!). They've even been active in recommending other nonprofits to donors if they think they aren't a good fit for that donor's needs or interests. This approach is revolutionary for our space. In an interview with *Christianity Today*, Horst and Greer said:

> *Cultivating humility, regardless of our age or stage in life, starts with a simple willingness to name our failures and shortcomings. We need to talk openly with*

others about the reasons we don't more actively partner and collaborate. As we take steps to acknowledge our need for others, we open the door to leading and serving others well — and truly, rooting for our rivals.

The mindset requires an unrelenting commitment to building trust and focusing on the greater good. Authentic collaboration with other nonprofits is hard. Failure is hard. Transparency with donors is hard. But the end result is a healthier organization that is free to operate out of an innovative growth mindset rather than falling back to what's always been done.

Keep in mind that when you use The Responsive Framework, many of your long-term risks and failures can be minimized and quickly fixed. Of course, the risk of failure always exists. But with data-driven decisions based on the behaviors and motivations of your donors, the risk of significant failure is mitigated. The Responsive Framework also gives you permission to quickly iterate and change as you learn. It admits that you don't know everything, and invites you to respond and connect differently as you learn.

Push your team to try new things — to pull inspiration from places outside of the nonprofit space. To talk to their colleagues and other professionals outside your organization. Leveraging community and relationships doesn't just help donor retention. It helps inspire your employees and reduce burnout when they feel supported and encouraged.

STAY CURIOUS

Finally, the most critical change to your organization is to always stay curious. One of the reasons nonprofits fell into this generosity crisis is because they didn't ask the right questions. Many nonprofits ask "how" to grow generosity, but fail to ask "why" donors continue to leave. Donor-centric fundraising requires relentless curiosity about the change your donors want to see in the world.

To execute The Responsive Framework, you are required to listen more. You must listen to all donor signals, including those that might not reveal positive feedback. Those signals should be the impetus for an investigation into how you can better serve your donors and, consequently, your cause. Remaining curious not only serves your employees and the culture of your organization, but most importantly, it supports the beneficiaries who you've dedicated yourself to.

THE FUTURE OF FUNDRAISING

A couple of years ago, my wife and I took our kids to pack meals with Feed My Starving Children. My wife and I give to a variety of charities, and while we talk openly to our children about the importance of giving and why it matters to us, we could see the detachment they felt to the act of writing a check. We wanted them to connect to the why behind our service, and Feed My Starving Children gave us that opportunity.

One of the best things about the organization is they ask for your time before they ever ask for financial donations. They want you to come to their facility, pack the meals, and get physically involved in the cause because they know how important that is to create connections between the donors and the beneficiaries.

As I watched my children carefully place items in the box, I witnessed them build a connection that could never be replicated in monetary giving. They started to understand that the bags of rice they placed in each box would be touched, prepared, and eaten by a malnourished and vulnerable child that might have been a classmate of theirs in different circumstances.

It's been a while since we've been back, but my kids still talk about the time we spent volunteering at Feed My Starving Children. What's remarkable about that is the fact that they are digital natives. They are Gen Z kids who don't know a world that isn't the hyper-connected, curated online universe. And yet, they thrived in an offline volunteering event. Because the truth is, it doesn't matter whether you are online or off. It doesn't matter if you're one person talking to 100,000 people or having a one-on-one conversation. People will respond to the same thing we have been responding to for the last 5,000 years: community and connection.

We want to be part of something. We want to help our neighbors and our friends. We want to serve each other in a way that is meaningful and makes the world a better place. Technology, behavior data, and changes in our experiences will never change that.

The future of giving is unknown. There may come a point in the not-so-distant future when cash is obsolete. It won't make sense for volunteers to stand outside stores in December ringing bells and collecting cash for The Salvation Army. Donations won't come in the form of checks in the mail. They might only come from online giving forms, text messages, or even crypto currency transfers directly to the frontlines of the cause.

We may continue the trend of globalization, expanding what it means to be part of a community. In the future, it may be almost impossible to gain momentum for causes that don't improve the world at large. Anything is possible at this point.

But what we do know for sure, what The Responsive Framework teaches us, is that if you focus on your community and their needs, you will be prepared for any revolution that comes. New technology will come and go, donor demands will evolve with each generation, and your nonprofit will be set up to ebb and flow with all of it.

Listen. Connect. Suggest. Those three steps will keep you engaged with your donors in a personal, meaningful way. Start today and future-proof your nonprofit for growth and impact. The world needs you.

ABOUT THE AUTHORS

GABE COOPER

Gabe Cooper is the Founder and CEO of Virtuous, a software platform helping nonprofits grow giving. He is also the founder of Brushfire Interactive and co-founder of Shotzoom, makers of GolfShot. Gabe has a true passion for creating market-defining software and helping charities reimagine generosity. After serving in a leadership role at a large nonprofit in the early 2000s, Gabe went on to help build a series of successful products in the nonprofit and for-profit sectors. His team's work has been featured by Apple, the *New York Times*, CNN, Mashable, *Forbes*, *USA Today*, and *Wired* magazine. Gabe, his wife Farrah, and their five kids live in Gilbert, Arizona.

MCKENNA BAILEY

Mckenna Bailey is a writer and strategist working to make empathy cool since 2012. Her other titles include *Play for a Living* and *We're Just Talking: The Simple Strategy to Mastering Any Job Interview*

TAKE THE NEXT STEP

Virtuous is the CRM and marketing platform designed to scale responsive fundaising for nonprofits.

Learn how Virtuous can be your partner in growing generosity and authentic donor relationships by visiting virtuouscrm.com.

STAY CONNECTED

Follow us on LinkedIn and Twitter @VirtuousCRM.

LEARN FROM THE EXPERTS

Hear responsive fundraisers offer insights, strategies and personal stories on The Responsive Fundraising Podcast. Available on Apple Podcasts, Spotify, or anywhere you listen to podcasts.

NOTES

NOTES

NOTES

NOTES